THE SACRED HEART OF JESUS

THE SACRED HEART OF JESUS

By
Mgr. Louis Gaston de Ségur

Translated from the French by
Ryan P. Plummer

LAMBFOUNT
St. Louis, Missouri

Published in 2024 by Lambfount · St. Louis, Missouri
www.lambfount.com

Mgr. Louis Gaston de Ségur, *The Sacred Heart of Jesus*, translated by Ryan P. Plummer.

The original French version was first published in 1872 by the Paris-based publisher Haton under the title *Mois du Sacré-Cœur: Le Sacré-Cœur de Jésus*.

English translation copyright © 2024 by Ryan P. Plummer

All rights reserved. Aside from the litanies and prayers at the end of this book, no part of this publication may be reproduced, distributed or transmitted in any form or by any means, including photocopying, recording, or other electronic or mechanical methods, without the prior written permission of the publisher, except in the case of brief quotations embodied in critical reviews and certain other noncommercial uses permitted by copyright law.

ISBN 978-1-7328734-3-8

Printing and manufacturing information for this book may be found on the final page.

Front cover image: Digitally modified reproduction of *Sacred Heart of Jesus* by Pompeo Batoni. Back cover image: Sketch of Mgr. Louis Gaston de Ségur as found in *The Illustrated Catholic Family Annual for 1883*, published in New York by The Catholic Publication Society Co.

Letter of our Most Holy Father Pope Pius IX to the author regarding this book

PIUS IX, POPE

D*EAR* S*ON*, G*REETINGS AND* A*POSTOLIC* B*LESSING.*

We congratulate you, dearest son, for your zeal and constant love for religion, which have moved you to publish a new work by means of which you intend, according to your own words, to render honor to the most holy Heart of Jesus, and to propagate its cult amongst the faithful. We do not doubt that this intention, already so praiseworthy in itself, is most pleasing to this divine Heart, which is our refuge and our consolation, and which favors with a very special love its adorers and the propagators of its glory.

As for the kind thought you had to offer Us this work for the eightieth anniversary of Our birth, We see in this a new proof of your great attachment to Us; We respond to it with equal affection and tenderness, and We heartily thank you for it.

Given in Rome, at St. Peter's, on 18 May 1872, in the twenty-sixth year of Our Pontificate.

PIUS IX, Pope

Contents

Preface   1

How a good faithful soul can sanctify the month of the Sacred Heart   3

I—How Our Lord Jesus Christ miraculously revealed the mystery of His Sacred Heart through Blessed Margaret Mary   9

II—Second revelation of the Sacred Heart to Blessed Margaret Mary   12

III—Third revelation of the Heart of Jesus   15

IV—Two other beautiful visions of the Sacred Heart granted to the same Blessed   19

V—Jesus's magnificent and consoling promises to the faithful devotees of the Sacred Heart   23

VI—That the demon has done everything to stop the establishment of the cult of the Sacred Heart of Jesus   26

VII—The seventeenth-century revelation of the Sacred Heart was not an unprecedented thing in the Church   31

VIII—Admirable designs of Providence in the revelation of the Sacred Heart   35

IX—On the ineffable and all divine excellence of the Most Sacred Heart of Jesus   40

X—That the Heart of Jesus is the living hearth of universal love   43

XI—How the Most Holy Trinity is living and reigning in the Heart of Jesus	46
XII—That the Heart of Jesus is the Temple, Altar, and Censer of divine love	49
XIII—How the Heart of Jesus is the life principle of the Man-God, the Mother of God, and the children of God	53
XIV—That the adorable Heart of Jesus is a furnace of love with regard to the Most Blessed Virgin Mary	56
XV—What the Heart of Jesus was for His holy Mother during His Passion	61
XVI—That the adorable Heart of Jesus is a furnace of love with regard to the Church triumphant, the Church militant, and the Church suffering	66
XVII—That the Divine Heart of Jesus is also a furnace of love with regard to each one of us	70
XVIII—That this love of the Redeemer is wondrously manifest in all the goods with which His Heart has filled us	73
XIX—That the Sacred Heart of Jesus loves us as His Father loves Him	76
XX—What the adorable Heart of Jesus suffered for us in His passion	81
XXI—The ineffable mercies of the Heart of Jesus in the sacrament of Penance	84
XXII—The Sacred Heart and the Blessed Sacrament	87

XXIII—How, in Holy Communion, the Heart of
Jesus purifies, illuminates, and deifies us in His
holy love 90

XXIV—That the Holy Ghost intimately unites our
hearts to the Sacred Heart of Jesus 94

XXV—An admirable example of this union of the
faithful soul with the Sacred Heart of Jesus 97

XXVI—That Jesus gives us His Heart to be our
heart 101

XXVII—That the adorable Heart of Jesus is our
refuge and our oracle 105

XXVIII—How the Sacred Heart is the model our
hearts must follow 108

XXIX—On the ineffable meekness of the Heart of
Jesus Christ 112

XXX—On the most profound humility of the divine
Heart of Jesus 116

XXXI—How much the Heart of Jesus shows itself
merciful to the little and the poor 120

XXXII—That the Immaculate Heart of Mary is but
one with the most adorable Heart of Jesus 123

XXXIII—The Sacred Heart of Jesus and France 127

Prayers 141
   Litany of the Sacred Heart of Jesus 142
   Litany of the Holy Heart of Mary 146
   Another Litany of the Holy Heart of Mary 150
   Act of Reparation to the Sacred Heart of Jesus 155
   Consecration to the Sacred Heart of Jesus 156

Preface

The purpose of this little work is to popularize the knowledge and therefore the love and worship of the Most Adorable and Most Sacred Heart of Our Lord Jesus Christ. I know, it is difficult to make truths of the mystical order understandable to everyone; in other words, it is difficult and most difficult to introduce simple minds and children to what one might call the core of our mysteries; but it is so desirable that this be done, that I am not afraid to undertake it in what concerns the Sacred Heart of Jesus, counting on the help of the Blessed Virgin, who loves the little, the humble, and the simple so much!

If I have the happiness of attaining my goal, this little book can be of great service to those thousands of holy priests, zealous missionaries, fervent religious, and good and pious mothers of families seeking through all means to make truly known, served, and loved around them the God of their heart and the Heart of their God.

We live in times when piety needs more than ever to be enlightened and strong, when doctrine is necessary to uphold love. Our Lord having presented His Heart to be the refuge of souls in the trials of the last times, this work seems to me to enter His merciful designs, and for this reason I dare to count on the blessing of Him for Whose love I undertake it.

A good number of the little chapters forming it have been inspired by an excellent work by a great servant of God of whom we shall soon speak, the venerable Fr. Eudes, one of the most apostolic priests of the seventeenth century. On fire with love for the Sacred Hearts of Jesus and Mary, he says wondrously beautiful and holy things of them in his treatise *The Admirable Heart of the Most Holy Mother of God*. This book is unfortunately forgotten today, and it is almost impossible to find a copy of it. I do not indicate the parts I have borrowed from it, because I wanted to allow myself the liberty to modify, abridge, and explain certain passages. So, if these little meditations do you some good, my dearest reader, it is to the good Fr. Eudes that you will often be indebted for them.

How a good faithful soul can sanctify the month of the Sacred Heart

The practice of consecrating an entire month to a certain one of the great devotions recommended by the Church cannot be too religiously observed. Of all the means for honoring, be it a mystery, or the Blessed Virgin, or a saint, this is certainly the simplest, the most practical, and the most accessible to all. This little exercise of piety that, for one month, is performed each day; this pious reading that presents us the same truth under all its aspects, permeates the soul little by little with the grace of the good God unto the soul's very depths—it is as a most gentle and continuous rain that penetrates the earth much more than a heavy storm rain that is most abundant but fleeting.

Thus, it is evident that the admirable institution of the month of Mary has contributed most powerfully to cultivating in the entire world devotion and love to the Blessed Virgin. There are parishes and there are families who owe their complete renewal to the month of Mary.

Besides the month of May, consecrated in this way to honor the Most Blessed Virgin, piety has consecrated the month of January to honoring the mysteries of the Holy Infancy of Jesus; the month of March to especially honoring St. Joseph; the month of July to venerating the mysteries of the Precious Blood; the month of November to practicing charity towards the poor souls in purgatory; and finally, the month of June to honoring more particularly the Most Holy and Most Adorable Heart of Jesus.[1]

---

[1] We give the month of the Sacred Heart *thirty-three days*, to honor the thirty-three years in the life of the Savior. The Holy See blessed

I dare to recommend to you, dear reader, to henceforth make the month of the Sacred Heart with as much exactitude and zeal as the month of Mary. The grace of the Sacred Heart is so excellent and so profoundly sanctifying, that you will most certainly draw from it great fruits of salvation.

If you cannot celebrate it in public, do so as a family, at a specific time when all the members of the family can be free; if you cannot do so as a family, do not fail at least to do so as an individual. However, I repeat, try to practice in common this excellent exercise of piety. When we pray together, we pray more efficaciously; we support and edify each other, we commit to punctuality, and while doing good to ourselves, we do good to others. We thereby practice charity, at the same time as piety, and we reap the fruit of the promise made by Our Lord to His disciples: *"For where there are two or three gathered together in my name, there am I in the midst of them"* (Mt 18:20).

This is then how I would advise you to worthily celebrate the month of the Sacred Heart, if you cannot do so in the church.

Before a crucifix, or better yet before a statue or image of the Sacred Heart, set up a kind of little altar, with some flowers and some candles. Guard against scorning these little things—they have a very great influence on piety, our souls almost always needing the help of the senses to apply ourselves to the things of God.

---

this thinking, granting beautiful indulgences to the Diocese of Nantes, where the devotion of the month of the Sacred Heart took this form.

If you can do so, keep lit for the entire month a small vigil lamp before the holy image, in honor of the adorable Heart of your Savior. Then, each day, most faithfully and on your knees, alone or with others, do your little exercise.

The simpler it is, the better. The modest work I offer you here will perhaps suffice for you. After you have recollected yourself for a moment, and after having religiously and holily made the sign of the cross, recite the Litany of the Sacred Heart that you will find at the end of this small book. If one understands Latin, it is much preferable to recite these kinds of prayers in Latin; Latin is the sacred language of the Church, and furthermore, it is incomparably more beautiful and more profound than French.

Then, read the little chapter for each day, and consecrate three or four minutes to really fathoming what you have read; to exciting in your heart sentiments of adoration, love, and repentance; and finally, to making one or two good resolutions.

To finish this little exercise of piety, you can profitably recite aloud each day the beautiful Litanies of the Holy and Immaculate Heart of Mary, the act of *reparation*, and the act of *consecration*, which you will also find at the end of this work. I have intentionally abridged these prayers, so that the daily exercise can conscientiously be made within a short quarter of an hour.

I dare also advise you to go to communion during this month of the Sacred Heart a little more often perhaps, and certainly with yet more fervor than usual. Do not forget that Friday is especially consecrated to the cult of the Sacred Heart, according to the formal order Our Lord

Himself gave, as we shall soon see, to His great servant Blessed Margaret Mary,[1] of the Visitation. If possible, you could do nothing better than go to communion each Friday of the month, especially to honor the Sacred Heart of Jesus and the mysteries of His love.

By piously honoring the Sacred Heart in this way, you will enter fully into the desires of the Sovereign Pontiff, of the Supreme Pastor of the sheep and lambs of Jesus Christ. "We desire nothing so much," he said very recently,[2] "We desire nothing so much as to see the faithful honor, under the symbol of His Most Sacred Heart, the charity of Jesus Christ in His Passion and in the institution of the Eucharist, to delight in these memories each day and to unceasingly renew its memory."

You will draw strength and consolation in this; and when you get up, you will be able to say with that good young woman laborer from Lyon who recently passed away in the odor of sanctity: "I consecrated myself to the Heart of Jesus. I asked of him asylum and protection. I told Him that He would always be my refuge.

"I told Him with all my heart: 'My good Jesus, my sweet Consoler, You Whom my heart loves and will never stop loving, I surrender to You this poor heart. You alone are its Master; You alone have the right to its love. I retire into the sanctuary of Your adorable Heart, and I never more want to go out from it. Do with me all that You will. In Your Heart, I shall find my consolation; in it, I shall

---

[1] St. Margaret Mary Alacoque was not canonized until 1920, which is why Mgr. de Ségur, writing decades prior, refers to her only as "Blessed" throughout this book.—Trans.

[2] Brief of Our Holy Father Pope Pius IX to the Bishop of Nantes, dated 27 September 1867.

pour out my heart when I have too many sorrows; in it, I shall go hide and lose myself entirely.'

"All my thoughts are for Jesus, for His Heart, for His august Sacrament."

This holy young girl innocently recounts that, even while sleeping, she did not go out from the Heart of her Jesus. "It has now been more than one year," she wrote, "that every night, without one exception, I have dreamed that I went to Holy Communion."

She went to communion every morning and led an angelic life. In her final illness, the desire for heaven absorbed her completely. "I wish to die," she said repeatedly. "I am homesick. Jesus Christ Himself is the heaven of the Angels and the Saints. O beautiful heaven, I still do not desire You enough!" She died as one predestined, at barely twenty-two years of age.[1]

Let us learn like her, at the feet of the Sacred Heart, the science of sciences, the one thing necessary, the science of true love, of true happiness.

---

[1] The quotations from this young Lyon woman are found in *Mon cher petit cahier, journal d'une jeune ouvrière* (Lyon: Josserand, 1870).—Trans.

I

How Our Lord Jesus Christ miraculously revealed the mystery of His Sacred Heart through Blessed Margaret Mary

Blessed Margaret Mary lived in France in the seventeenth century. She belonged to an honorable family of the magistracy of Burgundy. After having lived a very innocent youth much beset by all kinds of sorrows, she entered the Visitation of Paray-le-Monial (Diocese of Autun) in 1671 at twenty-three years of age, and died a most holy death there in 1690.

It was thus our France, Catholic France, which had the good fortune to inaugurate in the Church, with Rome's sovereign blessing, the public veneration of the Heart of Jesus. It was to Blessed Margaret Mary that went the honor of being the immediate cause of the feast that today gladdens all the faithful. In fact, Pius IX says in the decree of her beatification: "To establish this veneration that is so pious, so salutary, and so legitimate, and to spread it far and wide among men, it was Margaret Mary whom Our Lord deigned to choose."

He chose her by means of admirable, miraculous revelations the Church has recognized and which radiate the pure love of God.

It was in 1673. She had been a religious for two years; she was already accomplished in holiness, humility, charity, and all kinds of virtues. One day when she was in adoration before the Blessed Sacrament, quite happy having some free time a little more considerable than her multiplied occupations had left her, the Blessed felt herself enveloped by the presence of her God, and this so powerfully that she lost awareness of herself and of everything that was around her. "I abandoned myself," she said, "to this Divine Spirit, surrendering my heart to the power of His love.

"My Sovereign Master had me repose a long time on His divine chest, where He revealed to me the wonders of His love and the ineffable secrets of His Sacred Heart. He opened to me for the first time this Divine Heart in so real and so sensible a manner that He allowed me no room to doubt the truth of this grace.

"Jesus said to me: '*My Divine Heart is so full of love for men and for you in particular, My daughter, that, no longer able to contain within itself the flames of its blazing charity, it is necessary that it spread them by your means, and that it manifest itself to men to enrich them with the treasures it contains. I reveal to you the value of these treasures: they contain the graces of sanctification and salvation necessary to withdraw the world from the abyss of perdition. Despite your unworthiness and ignorance, I have chosen you for the fulfillment of this great design, so that it will be more manifest that it is I Who am doing everything!*'

"After these words, He asked me for my heart. I beseeched Him to take it, which He did. And He placed it in His adorable Heart, where He let me see it as a small atom that was being consumed in this blazing furnace. Then, drawing it out like a burning, heart-shaped flame, He put it back from where He had taken it, saying to me: '*Here, My beloved, is a precious pledge of My love; I have enclosed within your side a little spark of the most intense flames of this love, to serve as your heart, and to consume you until the final moment of your life. Its ardors shall not be extinguished.'*

"'*To leave you a sign that the grace I have just given you is not your imagination, and that it must be the foundation of all those graces I want to give you still, although I have closed the wound in your side, the pain from it will remain with you always. Until present you have only taken the name of My servant, I now give you that of Beloved Disciple of My Sacred Heart!*'"

The Blessed Sister added: "This such great favor lasted a long stretch of time. I did not know whether I was in heaven or on earth. For several days I remained as though fully inebriated, as though fully set on fire and so much outside of myself, that I could not bring myself to say a word. I could not sleep; for this wound, whose pain is precious to me, caused me such intense ardor that it consumed me and made be burn alive. I felt such a great fullness of God that I was unable to express it to my Superior as I would have wanted, despite the pain and confusion I feel in speaking of such favors.

"Since that day, every first Friday of the month, the Sacred Heart of my Jesus was shown to me as a sun, shining with a brilliant light, and whose all-burning rays beamed onto my heart; and I then felt ablaze with such an intense fire that I felt it was going to reduce me to ashes.

"It was particularly in those moments that my Divine Master gave me His lessons, and revealed to me the secrets of His adorable Heart."

And we also, despite our unworthiness, despite our misery, or rather even on account of this misery, we want to keep ourselves exposed to the beneficent rays of Your Most Holy Heart, Lord Jesus, our Savior! We want these divine flames to at last consume our lukewarmness; we want them to purify us of all our sins!

O Jesus, dew from heaven, flame of love and source of grace, burn, purify, and possess all my heart! O Divine Love, grow and reign within me; grow and reign everywhere on earth, as in the Paradise of the Blessed!

II

Second revelation of the Sacred Heart to Blessed Margaret Mary

"One day," said the Blessed Sister, "one day when the Blessed Sacrament was exposed, I felt drawn inside myself by an extraordinary recollection of all my senses and all my faculties. Jesus, my sweet Master, came to me all resplendent in glory, with His five wounds, burning like five suns. From this holy humanity exited flames from everywhere, but especially from that adorable chest, which resembling a furnace and having opened itself to my gaze, revealed to me His all-lovable Heart, which was the living source of these flames.

"He at the same time made known to me the ineffable wonders of His pure love, and to what excess He had borne this love towards men. He complained of their ingratitude and told me that this pain from His passion had been more keenly felt by Him than His other sufferings. *'If only they would make some return to me,'* He added, *'what I did for them would seem but little to My love. But they show Me only coldness, and they respond to My ardent attentions with only rejection. You, at least, My beloved daughter, give Me the consolation of making up for their ingratitude as much as you will be able to do so!'*

"And as I reminded Him of my powerlessness, He answered me: *'Behold, here is what is to make up for all that you lack.'* And at the same time, His Divine Heart having opened, there came from it such an ardent flame that I thought I was being consumed by it. I was entirely penetrated by it, and I could no longer bear it; I asked Him to have pity on my weakness. *'I shall be your strength,'* He said to me with kindness. *'Fear nothing. But be attentive to My voice and to what I ask of you to dispose yourself for the fulfillment of My designs.'*

"*'First, you will receive Me in Holy Communion as much as obedience will permit you, regardless of any mortifications and humiliations that may befall you for this—these are pledges of My love.'*

"*'Secondly, moreover, you will go to communion every first Friday of each month.'*

"*'Thirdly, every Thursday-to-Friday night, I will have you participate in that mortal sadness that I willed to experience in the Garden of Olives; and this participation in My sadness will reduce you to a kind of agony, more arduous to bear than death. You will accompany Me in that humble prayer that I then presented to My Father amidst all My anguish; and for this, you will rise between eleven o'clock and midnight, and you will remain prostrate with Me for one hour with your face to the ground, to appease the divine anger by asking mercy for sinners, as much as to honor and alleviate in some way the bitterness that I then felt from the abandonment of My Apostles, which obliged Me to reproach them for having been unable to watch one hour with Me. During this hour, you will do what I will teach you.'*

"And Jesus added: *'But listen, My daughter, do not heedlessly believe your mind, and do not trust it. Satan, furious with you, seeks to deceive you. This is why you are to do nothing without the approval of those guiding you, so that, finding you reliant on obedience, he cannot harm you; he has no power over the obedient.'*

"Throughout the time that this heavenly vision lasted, I no longer knew where I was. When it was over, I was completely outside myself, all burning and trembling. I could not hold myself up or speak."

Following this sacred apparition, the pain that the Blessed Sister continuously felt was so intense, the fire of love that inflamed her was so violent, that, no longer able to bear it, she fell ill from it and all but died. "The fire that was devouring me," she said, "threw me into a continuously high fever; but I had too much joy in suffering to complain about it. I did not speak of it, until my strength failed me. The fever lasted more than sixty days. Never did I feel so much consolation; for my entire body was suffering from extreme pains, and this alleviated a little bit the ardent thirst that I had to suffer, this divine fire only feeding on the wood of the cross, namely on all kinds of sufferings, scorn, humiliations, and pains. Everyone thought I was dying."

Instead of dying, she suddenly and supernaturally recovered, her Superiors having demanded of her this sign of the reality of the vision which she had had to make known to them by virtue of holy obedience. It was through the Blessed Virgin that Our Lord thus miraculously returned her health to her, or her life rather.

The Mother of God deigned to appear to her; she blessed her and consoled her for a long time; and as soon as she had left her, Sister Margaret Mary was able to get up, leave the infirmary, and resume the exercises of her rule. The entire Community witnessed with amazement freely walking the one who, a few hours before, seemed barely to have a breath of life.

The revelation of the mystery of the Sacred Heart thus received from the beginning the divine seal of certitude, the seal of the miracle.

With what profound faith and with what love should we not then honor, invoke, and adore the Divine Heart of Jesus!

III

Third revelation of the Heart of Jesus

Sister Margaret Mary however received a new and yet more significant grace regarding the Sacred Heart.

It was during the octave of the feast of Corpus Christi. The Blessed was in adoration in the monastery chapel. She felt herself extraordinarily urged to return her Savior love for love. Enraptured and outside herself, she saw Jesus revealing to her His Divine Heart. "*Behold,*" He said to her, "*behold this Heart which has loved men so much, that it has spared nothing, to the point of exhausting and spending itself, to testify its love to them.*

"*In return, I receive from most of them only ingratitude, through scorn, irreverence, sacrileges, and the coldness they have for me in this sacrament of love.*

"But what is yet more keenly felt by Me is that it is hearts consecrated to Me who treat Me this way.

"This is why I ask you that the first Friday after the octave of Corpus Christi be dedicated to celebrating a special feast to honor My Heart, making reparation to it and going to communion that day to atone for the unworthy treatment it has received during the time it has been exposed on altars. I promise you that My Heart will expand to abundantly spread the influences of its divine love over those who render it this honor and who work to have this honor rendered to it."

"But, my sweet Lord," Sister Margaret very confusedly replied to Him, "to whom are You addressing Yourself? To a creature so puny and a sinner so miserable that her unworthiness would be capable of preventing the fulfillment of Your design?"

The Divine Master replied to her, *"What, do you not know that I make use of the weakest subjects to confound the strong, and that it is ordinarily on the little and the poor in spirit that I show My power with greater brilliance, so that they attribute nothing to themselves?"*

"Then," the Blessed said, "give me the means to do what You command."

And Jesus added: *"Address yourself to My servant"* (this was Father de la Colombière, Sister Margaret Mary's director, a very holy religious of the Society of Jesus), *"and tell him on My behalf to do his utmost to establish this devotion, and to give this joy to My Heart."*

Instructed with this order by the Savior, the holy religious Father de la Colombière fervently obeyed. The Friday following the octave of Corpus Christi (it was 21 June 1675), he consecrated himself entirely as a victim of adoration and reparation to the adorable Heart of Jesus. He enlisted a great number of pious persons to do as much, and to faithfully practice the rules laid out by Our Lord to Sister Margaret Mary concerning very frequent communion and especially the communion of reparation on the first Friday of each month, as well as on the Friday following the octave of Corpus Christi. The effects of this holy practice were wondrous.

It is necessary that they also henceforth be so for us and in us. Yes, it is necessary that, to enter the merciful designs of Our Savior, we follow, we also, humbly and lovingly, the counsels He Himself deigned to give His blessed servant Margaret Mary.

First, we will stir up our spirit of faith, our zeal regarding the Divine Eucharist, and we will guard well against that neglect and irreverence of which Our Lord complained. Not only during the entire octave of Corpus Christi, but every time that He is exposed on the altar, every time that we assist at Benediction, that we hear Holy Mass, or even that we enter a church in which He reposes, we will carry ourselves in His presence with a most profound respect; we will adore Him with a humble heart, and we will make at His feet, from the bottom of our hearts, the reparation that He has expressly requested.

Secondly, we will henceforth go to communion more often and more piously than in the past. *"You will receive Me in Holy Communion as many times as obedience permits you."* These words of Jesus are for us, no less than for Blessed Margaret Mary. The Heart of our Jesus calls us all to the Holy Table. Oh, when will the day come when everyone hears this voice and understands this call? In the design of Jesus, as the Council of Trent says, repeating the words of St. Thomas, St. Augustine, and St. Ambrose, in Jesus's design, "the Eucharistic Bread is the daily Bread; it is received each day as a remedy for the infirmity of each day. Let us receive it then each day so that each day it benefits us. But let us live in such a way that we can receive it each day."[1] Such is the great practical rule of communion; such is the wish of the Church; such is the appeal of the Heart of Jesus. Let us bring to our spiritual father such a frankly good soul, so sincerely animated by good will and zeal for the service of Jesus Christ, so that he can give us this consoling directive: "Go, my child, go in all confidence, and receive daily, if possible, the God of your heart." How much the face of the world would change if many souls were to resolutely embark upon this path of benediction, love, fervor, and salvation!

Finally, according to the command of our sweet Master, we will consecrate the first Friday of each month in a very special way to reparative adoration; and we will do on this day, in a spirit of penitence and humility, the communion requested by Jesus of all the "disciples of His Sacred Heart."

---

[1] Panis iste quotidianus sumitur in remedium quotidianæ infirmitatis. Quotidie ergo sume, ut quotidie tibi prosit. Sic vive, ut quotidie merearis accipere (*Cat. Rom. ad parochos*).

IV

Two other beautiful visions of the Sacred Heart granted to the same Blessed

Sister Margaret Mary was one day in a small courtyard of the monastery, adjacent to the chapel in which the Most Blessed Sacrament reposed. She was there on her knees doing the work with which she had been tasked. She was by a hazel tree that they still show at Paray-le-Monial.

"I felt fully recollected interiorly and exteriorly," she said in the memoir where she continuously noted out of obedience the supernatural favors of which she was the object. "And I saw, more resplendent than the sun, the Heart of my adorable Jesus. It appeared as surrounded by flames; and these flames were those of His love. It was surrounded by Seraphim, who in admirable unison chanted: 'Love triumphs!... The love in God rejoices.'

"These blessed spirits invited me to unite myself with them in this canticle of praises to the Heart of Jesus Christ; but I did not dare do so. They reproved me and told me that they had come to render with me to this Sacred Heart a perpetual homage of love, adoration, and praise; that for this, they would hold my place before the Blessed Sacrament, so that through their mediation, I could love and adore Him without interruption; that they would participate in suffering love in my person, just as in their persons I would participate in triumphant love. At the same time, they seemed to me to write in letters of gold this association in the Sacred Heart, with the indelible characters of love.

"This lasted about two or three hours. All my life I have felt the effects of this, as much by the help I have received from this mysterious association as by the sweetness it has produced in me and that it produces in me still.

"I remained all immersed in confusion. However, in praying to these holy Angels, I called them only my divine associates. This grace gave me such a great desire for purity of intention, it gave me such a lofty idea of what is needed to converse with God, that everything seemed impure to me when compared to the fervor of the Seraphim."

Alas, if only you were there for us as for her, O burning Seraphim, most pure and most perfect adorers of the Sacred Heart of our God! But I stand corrected: you are there, you are always there! Day and night you adore, for us and with us, in heaven and before the Blessed Sacrament, this Lord Jesus, your King and ours, your Love and our Love, your Light and our Light. What you do invisibly, we do visibly; what you do in the beatitude of heaven, we do, or alas, we at least ought to do, amidst the earth's struggles and miseries. Oh, make up for the infirmity of our adoration! If a special pact should bind you to this or that specific individual among us, as to your Blessed "Associate," there nevertheless reigns between you and us, between the Church of heaven and the Church of earth, a very close union, an intimate and indissoluble union. Come then, come to help us, blessed Seraphim, blessed Cherubim, Angels, and Archangels of the nine heavenly choirs! Come, let us adore Jesus! Let us adore Him together in the mystery where both His love and His sacrifice triumph; and with one heart, let us adore, love, and exalt His Sacred Heart. *Venite adoremus!*

Sister Margaret Mary again had the happiness of contemplating, in a no less splendid vision, the Divine Heart of which she was to be the apostle in the Church. On 27 December 1686, the feast day of St. John the Evangelist, at the moment she was going to communion, Our Lord wanted to reveal to her once more the mysteries of His sacred love.

"The Heart of Jesus was represented to me," she said, "as in a throne formed by fire and flames, radiating from all sides, more brilliant than the sun and transparent like a crystal. The wound it received on the cross visibly appeared there. There was a crown of thorns around this Sacred Heart, and on top a cross which seemed implanted in it.

"My Divine Master made me understand that these instruments of His Passion signified that the immense love of His Heart for men had been the source of all His sufferings; that from the first instant of His Incarnation all these torments had been present to Him; and that from that first moment the cross was, so to speak, planted in His Heart; that He accepted from that moment all the pains that His holy humanity would suffer during the course of His mortal life, as well as all the outrages to which His love for men would expose Him until the end of the ages, while dwelling with them in the Blessed Sacrament."

And Jesus added: *"I have a burning thirst to be honored and loved by men in the Blessed Sacrament; and yet I find almost no one who endeavors, according to My desire, to quench this thirst by making Me some return of love."*

Sister Margaret Mary tells us that this loving complaint from the Savior pierced her soul. Oh, may it then pierce ours also! May it sway, like an irresistible wind sways large trees, may it sway, may it shake, may it awaken all priests, ministers of the Eucharist, dispensers of the holy mysteries! And may it make them understand what many do not understand enough, namely, the insatiable desire Jesus has to see all His children flocking to the Holy Table and crowding around the altars to there receive adorable Communion! On this account the Savior confides to them this dear desire of His Heart, and He fully leaves it to their love, their zeal, and their fidelity.

O blessed is the priest whose single care consists in making known to souls Jesus in the Eucharist! To exciting them all to communicate piously and often, "*sancte ac frequenter*," as the Church says;[1] to communicating very often, and every day even, if possible. Blessed and a thousand times blessed is the truly prudent and faithful servant who answers the wishes of his good Master, by giving with a holy mercy the Bread of Life to the children of God! Piety and fervor will blossom around him: feeding on Jesus, children will easily preserve their innocence; young men and young women, the virginal beauty of their souls; families, the solemn and sweet sanctity of the domestic hearth; holy vocations, good works, the zeal of faith, and charity towards the unfortunate will develop as if by enchantment; in a single word, everything that is good and beautiful here below, this blessed priest will see it multiply around him, as a pledge of his eternal crown.

---

[1] *Rituale Rom., de Eucharistia.*

Oh, let us ask the Heart of Jesus to give to His Church more and more priests ardently devoted to the heavenly interests of the Blessed Sacrament, priests whose supreme joy is to give Jesus to souls, to all souls, so that Jesus truly lives and reigns in them. Let us never forget that this is the most ardent wish of His Sacred Heart.

V

Jesus's magnificent and consoling promises to the faithful devotees of the Sacred Heart

In the beautiful vision we just recounted, in which Our Lord had Sister Margaret Mary contemplate His Sacred Heart amidst a burning light on a mysterious and resplendent throne, He left to her, for all souls who would devote themselves to the veneration of this adorable Heart, promises that are as consoling as they are sanctifying. Let us engrave them on our souls and meditate on them with a love full of gratitude.

Jesus therefore said to the Blessed: *"The great desire that I have to be loved perfectly by men made Me resolve to manifest to them My Heart, and to give them in these last times this last effort of My love, by offering them an object and a means so apt for enlisting them to love Me, to solidly loving Me."* – Notice that the Sacred Heart is given to us as an extreme remedy in extreme dangers: the dangers of the last times. *"For there shall be then,"* the Gospel says, *"great tribulation, such as hath not been from the beginning of the world until now... The powers of heaven shall be moved... Many shall be deceived... And unless the Lord had shortened the days, no flesh should be saved; but for the sake of the elect which He hath chosen, He hath shortened the days."*[1] Now, what is and will be for us the great means of preservation and salvation? Jesus Himself deigns to teach this to us: it is His adorable and adored Heart, the *"last effort of His love in these last times."* And how will the loving veneration of His divine Heart save us? By inciting us *"to love Him, to solidly loving Him."* One can assert without fear that "the elect," the true Christians of the Church in the last times, will be the faithful of the Sacred Heart of Jesus.

The Savior further said: *"In giving them My Heart, I open to them all the treasures of love, grace, sanctification, and salvation that this Heart contains, so that all those who want to render and procure for it all the love and honor that will be possible for them may be profusely enriched by the treasures of which this Divine Heart is the source, the fecund and inexhaustible source. I will write their names on My Heart, and I will never permit them to be effaced from it."* – "All those who want," and who is he who would not want? "All the treasures of love, grace, mercy, sanctification, and salvation"—What promises! What goodness! Oh, who would be a great enough enemy to himself that he would not open his heart to the voice of Jesus Christ?

Responding in advance to the criticisms of the Jansenists, the rebellious, and even certain ill-advised Christians, Our Lord then said to Blessed Margaret Mary:

"I take a singular satisfaction in seeing the interior sentiments of My Heart and of My love honored in the

---

[1] Mt 24:21, 22, 29; Mk 13:6, 20.

figure of this Heart of flesh, such as I have shown it to you, and I want its image to be exposed in public, in order to touch the insensitive heart of man. I will abundantly spread, over the hearts of those who will honor it, the treasures of grace with which My Heart is filled; and everywhere this image will be exposed to be specially honored, it will draw down all kinds of blessings." – Therefore, let us have in our home, and let us carry on us, some pious image of this Most Sacred Heart of Jesus; and let the worldly talk. Is it not a hundred times better to obey and please Jesus rather than men?

Finally, the blessed confidante of the mysteries of the Sacred Heart summed up in this way, in a letter she wrote a few years before her death, the wondrous benefits of devotion to the Heart of Jesus:

"I do not know there to be, in the spiritual life, any exercise of devotion more capable of raising a soul to the highest sanctity in a short time, and of having it taste the veritable sweetness of God's service.

"Yes, I say this with certainty: if one only knew how much this devotion pleases Jesus Christ, there is not a Christian, however little love he might have for this lovable Savior, who would not practice it immediately.

"Secular persons will find through this means all the help necessary for their state, meaning peace in their families, relief in their work, and heaven's blessings on all their undertakings. It is rightly in this adorable Heart that they will find a place of refuge during their life, and principally at the hour of their death. Oh, how sweet it is to die after having had a constant devotion to the Sacred Heart of Him Who is to judge us!"

As for religious and priests, here are the magnificent promises which especially concern them: "My Divine

Savior made me to understand that those who work for the salvation of souls will have the art of touching the most hardened hearts, and will work with a wondrous success, if they themselves are penetrated with a tender devotion to His Divine Heart.

"May men and women religious embrace this sanctifying devotion—they will draw from it such help that no other means will be needed to reestablish the original fervor and the most exact regularity in the least well-regulated Communities, and to bring to the fullness of perfection the Communities already living in the most exact regularity."

Let each one of us take to heart what the Blessed Sister says in concluding her letter: "There is no one in the world who would not experience all kinds of help from heaven if he had for Jesus Christ a grateful love, such as the love one bears witness to Him through devotion to His Sacred Heart."

VI

That the demon has done everything to stop the establishment of the cult of the Sacred Heart of Jesus

The more the cult of this adorable Heart was excellent and profitable to souls, the more the demon had to fear it and stop its establishment by all possible means. For this purpose, he made use of a new sect, born from Calvinism, and which soon, under the name of *Jansenism*, took on in France grievous proportions.

Under the pretext of penance and austerity, and under the pretext of a more perfect return to the primitive traditions of Christianity, the Jansenists virulently attacked as much as they could anything in Religion that was consoling and merciful: frequent communion, trust in the divine mercy, love and veneration of the Blessed Virgin, and the splendors of divine worship. These icy-hearted heretics, with love for neither God nor men, could not countenance a devotion so imbued with love, as was the devotion to the Sacred Heart. In a series of abominable schemes, slanderous defamations, and more or less open persecutions, they made desperate efforts to suffocate in its crib the nascent devotion to the Sacred Heart of Jesus. They tried to portray it as superstitious, absurd, ridiculous, and impious. They wanted to incite against it the clergy, the faithful, and even certain doctors on theology faculties. They sought to deceive the bishops; they brought the calumnies all the way to Rome; they tried provoking King Louis XIV and the Court against it, and momentarily succeeded in this. The sectarians' anger was principally directed against the Jesuit Order, which, ever on fire for the sanctification of souls, had embraced with a love much worthy of it the devotion to the Sacred Heart. The poor Sister Margaret Mary was derided; and her magnificent revelations, though fully tested and approved by the competent authority, these revelations that Our Lord had confirmed through miracles, they were deemed fantasies.

But prior to this, the anger of the demon and of the Jansenists had been focused on a holy missionary whom Providence had raised up to prepare the way for Blessed Sister Margaret Mary, and for the revelation itself of the mysteries of the Heart of Jesus. It was the venerable Father Eudes, a disciple of Cardinal de Bérulle and of

Father de Condren, and a friend of St. Vincent de Paul, of the holy Father Olier, and of everything eminent and virtuous that the seventeenth-century clergy comprised. For over fifty years, this admirable priest, whom Father Olier called the "the wonder of his century," filled nearly all of France with his apostolic preaching, and propagated all over the country, with an inspired fervor, the love and cult of the Holy Hearts of Jesus and Mary. This was his great devotion; he communicated it not only to the people, but to the clergy and religious congregations. With the approval of the bishops and under their patronage, he founded a congregation of missionaries (the *Eudist* Fathers), specially devoted to this cult of love; he founded seminaries, public chapels, and numerous flourishing confraternities which the Holy See itself approved through official acts, and this at the same time when, in the silence of the monastery of Paray-le-Monial, Jesus was beginning to miraculously reveal Himself, as we have seen, to Blessed Margaret Mary.

He also, the good Fr. Eudes, can therefore and must be called "the apostle of the Heart of Jesus." From the year 1645, he had the happiness of having solemn veneration rendered to the Sacred Heart in the seminaries of his congregation and in many religious houses; and in 1671, the Archbishop of Rouen and the Bishops of Rennes, Coutances, Lisieux, Évreux, Bayeux, and Autun approved and authorized in their dioceses, always at the entreaties of Fr. Eudes, devotion to the Sacred Heart of Jesus; they permitted its feast to be publicly celebrated with a proper Mass and Office. This Mass and this Office, which are admirable, were the work of the pious missionary. The Holy See twice approved them; and the

Eudist Fathers still today have the good fortune of making use of them. In the year 1674, whilst Our Lord was magnificently revealing Himself to Blessed Margaret Mary, His Vicar, Pope Clement X, gave, through six Apostolic Briefs, the Holy See's supreme approval to the legitimacy of the cult of the Sacred Heart.

The demon, more furious than ever, raged against Fr. Eudes. He took advantage of the holy missionary's truly priestly attitude in the nascent Gallican disputes, which, as everyone knows, were born of Jansenist intrigues. The noble defender of the rights of the love of Jesus Christ and of the authority of His Vicar had the glory of suffering exile and persecution. He died at [no] more than eighty years of age, in the odor of sanctity; and the cause of his beatification is now before the Sacred Congregation of Rites.[1]

One can see that the apostolate of Fr. Eudes was like the pedestal for the revelations in Paray-le-Monial, and the immediate preparation for the marvels that the Son of God was going to work through His humble and very holy servant Sister Margaret Mary.

Jansenism's fury could not prevent God's work from growing and planting deep roots in pious souls. But it often succeeded in producing in many other souls, quite good souls incidentally, regrettable prejudices concerning devotion to the Sacred Heart. Even today, there are some who tell you in very good faith that the cult of the Sacred Heart is a childish thing, a thing fit for impressionable women, a thing unworthy of Christian piety, which must

---

[1] St. John Eudes (1601-1680) died at age seventy-eight. He was beatified in 1909 and canonized in 1925.—Trans.

always have something somber and austere; that there are no more reasons to render a special veneration to the Heart of Our Lord than to His head, His hands, His feet, etc.; that the worship of the Blessed Sacrament quite suffices since we have there Our Lord in His entirety; that the Heart of Our Lord is inseparable from His body, and lastly, that the image of a heart of flesh is hardly appealing.

Unfortunately for these reasoners, Our Lord and His Church are not of their opinion. The image of the material Heart of Jesus was indicated and requested by Our Lord Himself; and it must be believed that He knows better than us what He is doing. The Church has officially and solemnly proclaimed, through the mouths of Sovereign Pontiffs, the excellence of the cult of the Sacred Heart, and in particular of those images so unjustly incriminated. This cult that is so sweet, and so profoundly Christian and sanctifying, has long been not only proposed, but imposed on the Church through the Catholic liturgy; and inasmuch as these perils of the "last times" of which the Savior spoke to Blessed Margaret Mary increase, one sees devotion to the Sacred Heart taking on more consoling proportions each day. Parishes, dioceses, and entire countries are publicly consecrated to the Divine Heart of Jesus. Conversions and graces without number everywhere accompany this all-loving devotion.

And I also, my most holy and most sweet Savior, I also want to dedicate and devote myself entirely to Your adorable Heart! Fill me with the spirit of Your Church, which is Your Holy Spirit, Your Spirit of Love. It is in Him, it is in His divine light that I want to learn to know You, to adore You, to pray to You, to serve You, to win

You hearts, to console You for so much ingratitude, and to make up to You for so much forgetfulness! It is He Who unites me to Your Divine Heart; it is He Who makes me dwell in You, both in time and in eternity.

VII

The seventeenth-century revelation of the Sacred Heart was not an unprecedented thing in the Church

The Jansenists criticized the cult of the Sacred Heart for being a "novelty and something without precedent." That was not true.

In fact, four centuries prior to the apostolate of Fr. Eudes and the revelations of Blessed Margaret Mary, the celebrated Benedictine abbess St. Gertrude had received revelations from Our Lord, no less magnificent than those of Paray-le-Monial, concerning the Sacred Heart. Jesus had even ordered her to put them in writing: "*You will not leave this world,*" He told her one day that her humility was making her hesitate, "*you will not leave this world, until you have finished writing. I require it. I want your writings to be, for the last times, a pledge of My divine goodness. Through them, I will do good to a great number of faithful. Whilst you write, I will hold your heart close to Mine, and I will instill in it, drop by drop, what you must say.*" And St. Gertrude's admirable book forever established her as the most intimate evangelist of the Sacred Heart of Jesus.

On the feast of St. John, the disciple whom Jesus loved was shown to St. Gertrude in the splendor of an incomparable glory. "My most loving Lord," the blessed woman said to Jesus Christ, "why do you present to me, an unworthy creature, your dearest disciple?" – "*I want,*" Jesus replied, "*to establish between him and you an intimate friendship—he will henceforth be in heaven your faithful protector.*"

Then, addressing Gertrude, St. John said to her: "Come, Spouse of my Master, together let us repose our heads on the Lord's most sweet chest; in it are contained all the treasures of heaven."

And St. Gertrude having leaned her head on the right side of the Savior's chest as St. John rested his head on the left side, the beloved disciple continued: "Here is the Holy of Holies; all the goods of earth and heaven are drawn here as towards their center."

The beatings of the Heart of Jesus enraptured the soul of Gertrude. "Beloved of the Lord," she asked St. John, "these harmonious beatings, which rejoice my soul, did they rejoice yours when you reposed, during the Last Supper, on the Savior's chest?" – "Yes," the Apostle replied, "yes, I heard them, and their sweetness penetrated to the depths of my soul." – "Why is it then that in your gospel you have barely hinted at the loving secrets of the Heart of Jesus Christ?" – "My ministry in that first era of the Church had to be confined to speaking about the uncreated Word, the eternal Son of the Father, and some fecund words that the intellect of men could always meditate upon without ever exhausting their riches, but in the last times has been reserved the grace to hear the eloquent voice of the beatings of the Heart of Jesus; at this voice the aged world will rejuvenate: it will exit from its torpor, and the warmth of divine love will again enflame it."

In another place in her book, Gertrude makes us to hear these beatings of the Heart of Jesus Christ as an echo. The Saint saw her Sisters hastening to go to the church to be present for the sermon; and illness kept her in her cell. "Oh, my dearest Lord," she said sighing, "how I would gladly go to the sermon if I were not ill." – "*My beloved, do you want Me to preach to you Myself?*" Our Lord immediately responded. – "Very much so," Gertrude simply replied. Then Jesus inclined the soul of Gertrude towards His Sacred Heart, and she soon discerned there two beatings most sweet to hear. "*One of these beatings,*" Jesus said to her, "*works the salvation of sinners; the other, the sanctification of the just.*

"*The first speaks unceasingly to My Father, in order to appease His justice and to draw His mercy. Through this same beating, I speak to all the Saints, excusing sinners before them, with the indulgence and zeal of a good brother, and urging them to intercede for them. This same beating is the incessant appeal I mercifully address to sinners themselves, with an indescribable desire to see them return to Me, Who never tire of waiting for them.*

"*Through the second beating, I continually say to My Father how much I am pleased to have given My blood to redeem so many just, in the hearts of whom I taste joys without number. I invite the heavenly court to admire with Me the lives of these perfect souls, and to render thanks to God, for all the good He prepares for them. Finally, this beating of My Heart is the habitual and familiar conversation I have with the just, whether to delightfully testify My love to them, or to correct them for their faults, and to make them progress day by day, hour by hour.*

"No external occupation, no distraction of sight nor of hearing, interrupts the beatings of the heart of man; similarly, the providential governance of the universe could not, until the end of time, stop, interrupt, or slow down, even for an instant, these two beatings of My Heart."

One day, holding His Divine Heart in His hands, Jesus presented it to St. Gertrude and said to her: *"Behold My most sweet Heart, the harmonious instrument whose chords enrapture the Holy Trinity! I give it to you; and like a faithful and attentive servant, it will be at your command, to supply for your powerlessness. Make use of My Heart, and your works will charm the gaze and the ear of God."*

Gertrude lived in this way on love, tenderness, and sacrifices in the Sacred Heart of her God, until her final breath. At the time of her death, on 17 November 1292 [1302], the Sister to whom the holy abbess had dictated her book saw Our Lord appear close to the dying one. The Savior's face was beaming with joy; at His right stood the Blessed Virgin; at His left, the beloved Apostle, St. John. Around them were gathered a multitude of Angels, Virgins, and Saints.

Near the dying one's bed was read the Gospel of the Passion. At the words *"bowing His head, He gave up the ghost,"* Jesus leaned towards Gertrude; with His two hands He opened His own Heart halfway and radiated its flames into the blessed one's soul.

A few moments before she expired, Jesus lovingly said to her: *"Finally, the moment has come to give your soul the kiss that is to unite it to Me! Finally, My Heart can present you to My heavenly Father!"*

And immediately, the blessed soul of Gertrude, breaking the bond that attached it to her body, rose luminously towards Jesus, and entered the sanctuary of His most sweet Heart.

It was this same mystery of love, mercy, and sanctification that Jesus would reveal four hundred years later, as we said, to be "in the last times, the pledge of His divine goodness."

Let us adore Him and bless Him with our whole heart.

VIII

Admirable designs of Providence in the revelation of the Sacred Heart

The good God does everything in His time. His wisdom united itself to His mercy in giving to the Church the divine treasure of the Heart of Jesus for the time when it was going to have the greatest need of it. The Savior said so Himself, first to St. Gertrude and then to Blessed Margaret Mary: "My Divine Heart is destined for the last times."

Let there be no mistake, all the signs indicated by the Son of God in the twenty-fourth chapter of St. Matthew amass and unite, so to speak, with fearful evidence: the faith diminishes and goes away; the Gospel is preached almost everywhere; baptized societies have all apostatized; frightful wars and struggles of people against people and nation against nation terrify the world over;

miracles spring up everywhere; a truly extraordinary mass of prophecies, many of which are certainly authentic, unite holy souls by a secret instinct; finally, the three mysteries which seemingly must serve as a refuge for the Church of God in the supreme tribulations, the mystery of the infallibility of the Pope, the mystery of the Immaculate Conception of Mary, and the mystery of the Sacred Heart of Jesus, tower over the universal tempest incited against all that is Catholic, bringing the true faithful the steadfastness of faith and obedience, the grace of innocence necessary for triumph, and the gift of absolutely divine charity, mercy, and reparation. Everything signals to us the more or less immediate approach of these "last times" predicted by the God of the Sacred Heart.

In the preceding ages, for each new malady that was declared, the Savior immediately drew a salutary remedy "from the good treasury of His Heart"; in our age, in which all negations and old maladies are going to concentrate and more and more ally themselves under the banner of *Revolution* and anti-Christianism, it is His very Heart, it is the treasury with everything it contains, that Jesus deigns to open to us and give to us in its entirety. This is the last effort of His love; it is the supreme and universal remedy.

Yes, the Sacred Heart is what the Church *requires* in these extraordinary times. For an extreme evil, it is necessary to have an extreme remedy, a remedy beyond which there would be nothing further. Baptized Europe, particularly France, has rotted to its heart; thus, to escape death, the faithful must draw life from the source, by entering the Heart of the King of Heaven. The more things progress, the more it will be true to say: "Outside the Heart of Jesus, there is no salvation."

One thus perceives the merciful designs of Providence, which delayed the manifestation of the Sacred Heart until the end of the seventeenth century, until the time when Satan was going to stir up Voltaire, Rousseau, Freemasonry, philosophical atheism, and finally the Revolution itself, meaning the great Revolt of society against the Church, of man against the Son of Man, and of earth against heaven.

At the end of the seventeenth century, Calvinism and Jansenism wanted to suppress, one in theory and the other in practice, the sacrament of love, and consequently love itself, holy and confident love, which is born from communion. In opposition to the Pharisees of the last times, Jesus sets the revelation of His adorable Heart, all superabundant with meekness and humility, an inexhaustible source of tenderness, charity, mercy, true holiness, and true love. And as the evil was coming from France, from this noble and beautiful France destined to protect and propagate the Church, it is in France that most wise Providence brings about the remedy by manifesting the mysteries of the Sacred Heart.

The impious of the eighteenth century are going to make their satanic cry heard, their war cry against Jesus Christ, Whom they want to exterminate: *"Let us crush the infamous one!"* They, through their sophisms and through their infernal and universal propaganda, are going to unsettle minds. What is Jesus Christ going to do? He Who made man and Who knows man, He goes right to the heart of man and manifests Himself to him under the most powerful, most intimate, and most alluring form: as

Sovereign Love. He gives him His Divine Heart; and through the heart He pulls him from the mortal seductions of the mind. Indeed, nothing is stronger than love; and through the revelation of His Sacred Heart, Jesus will make Himself loved. Oh, the beautiful ruse of war!

That is not all. Great crimes are going to be born from these great blasphemies: the conspiracy of anti-Christian Freemasonry is going to shake the Church to its foundations; a savage persecution is going to destroy Europe's ancient Catholic institutions, and, appropriately beginning by way of France and Rome, it is going to chop off the head less of the most Christian king than of the most Christian monarchy, less of Louis XVI than of the eldest son of the Church; it is going to close the temples, massacre the priests and bishops, destroy the religious orders, raise a harlot above the altars, drag the Pope into exile and have him die therein; it is going to inaugurate a new society without faith, without God, without Jesus Christ; it is going to inaugurate and propagate throughout the entire world that immense blasphemy called the separation of Church and State; it is going to ruin the life of grace in millions and millions of souls.

To these crimes, which necessarily call down the retribution of divine justice, to these public and heretofore unprecedented sacrileges, Our Lord Jesus Christ brings an expiation whose holiness surpasses and will always surpass human perversity: He reveals and inaugurates the public cult of His Sacred Heart; and this cult, a thousand times blessed, essentially expiatory and reparative, is going to propagate itself in such a way that "where sin abounds, grace more abounds" still. Though Satan may inspire as much as he wants the human-faced demons who, for more than a hundred years, have made the world resound with their blasphemies, and who insult and trample the most holy and most adorable Eucharist, though he have them blaspheme the Blessed Virgin, kill priests, and commit all their crimes, though he do so, the Church henceforth has a means of reparation, more powerful than all the levers of hell. It has the Most Sacred Heart of Jesus, the Heart of God Himself.

For these reasons, and for yet others still, which would take too long to expound upon here, most merciful Providence was admirable in revealing the cult of the Sacred Heart at the end of the seventeenth century.

Let us add that when the Blessed Virgin appeared on 19 September 1846 on the mountain of La Salette, in order to save, if possible, her poor France, and through France Rome and the Church, she declared among other things that the propagation of the cult of the Sacred Heart would be one of the means of which the good God would make use to combat anti-Christianism and to sanctify His faithful, His elect of the last times. This revelation contributed not a little to propagating everywhere the love and veneration of the Sacred Heart.

Let us enter this current of faith—it is the way of salvation. Let us listen to the voice of the Church; let us listen to the warnings of the Blessed Virgin; let us believe and accept with love the words of Our Lord Himself. Yes, the Sacred Heart is the mystery of these last times.

However, so that the ineffable excellences of the Sacred Heart better penetrate us, and consequently the excellence of the cult and devotion rendered to it in the Church, let us contemplate more closely, with the eyes of faith, with the happiness and joy of divine love, this most loving, most loved, and a thousand times adorable Heart of Our Lord Jesus Christ.

May He forever be the King of our hearts.

IX

On the ineffable and all divine excellence of the Most Sacred Heart of Jesus

The world is composed of two kinds of creatures: spirits and bodies. Outside of God, Father, Son, and Holy Ghost, the Creator of the universe, there exist only the world of spirits and the world of bodies.

Now, the world of spirits is created by God according to a type, a perfect model, which is as its center; and this type, this exemplar, is the most holy soul that the eternal Son of God deigned to unite to Himself when He became man, in the midst of time. It was in the image and likeness of this sacred soul that the good God, for Whom everything is present, created in the beginning all the angels as well as the souls of our first parents. It was in the image and likeness of His Son that He created and that He continues to create all our souls.

It is the same for the world of bodies, for the world of matter: the adorable body that the Son of God was to one day take in the womb of the Virgin was the type, the model after which the good God created first the world and then man, the king of the world. Yes, the body of Adam was made, in the earthly paradise, after the model of the most perfect body that the Son of God was to unite one day to His soul and to His divine person.

The humanity of Jesus Christ is thus, in the plan of creation, as the center and reason for being of all creatures, principally of angels and men.

To express the excellences of this humanity that has become the humanity of the Son of God, of this soul and of this body so united to the eternal person of this same Son of God, that, without confusing themselves in the least with His divinity, form with it a single and unique divine, eternal, and infinite person, is an absolutely impossible thing. Never, neither in this world nor in the other, will we be able to fully comprehend the *infinite* mystery of Jesus Christ; never will we be able to adore Him as perfectly as He deserves; never will we be able to admire, love, and bless Him as much as He deserves to be blessed, loved, and admired.

The humanity of God! A created soul and a created body, having become the soul and body of God Himself, and hence *adorable and divine!...* What an abyss of grandeurs! What a mystery!!

Indeed, in this adorable and all divine humanity, there is something more extra-adorable still, if it is permitted to speak in such a way; in this abyss of holiness and majesty, there is something more holy, more sublime, and more excellent: it is the Heart of Our Lord, Creator, and Redeemer Jesus Christ. Yes, in the most adorable humanity of our God, we must put above everything His Most Sacred Heart.

In Jesus Christ, as in us, the *heart* is in effect the most noble and most delicate organ. It is as the summary and, so to speak, the living center and core of the entire body. The soul, which animates the body and exercises its various faculties through the various organs of the body, exercises through the *heart* the most sublime of all its faculties, the faculty of *loving*. The soul thinks through the brain and in union with the brain, and it senses through the nerves, which extend into all our senses; but it is through the heart, and through the heart alone, that it loves. From this, the supereminent excellence of the heart; from this also, the language universally used among men, and employed by the Holy Ghost in divine Scripture, in which the heart is presented as the summary of the person. To have a good heart is to be good; to have an evil heart is to be evil. To have heart is to be generous and devoted; to be heartless is to be selfish, it is to be evil. The heart is the whole man, contemplated in what is most excellent in him.

Now, I repeat, it is the same in this unique divine Man Who is God, Who is Jesus Christ. The *heart* of Jesus Christ is, if we may express ourselves this way, what is most divine and most ineffable in His most divine and most ineffable body. His heart is the living organ of His love; and His love is the infinite love of God incarnate!

O holy humanity of my Savior! O holy and most holy Heart of my adorable Jesus! I love You with all the powers of my soul, and with my face to the ground I prostrate myself before You!

X

That the Heart of Jesus is the living hearth of universal love

In 1670, the venerable Bishop of Évreux, approving for his diocese the cult of the Sacred Heart and the Office composed for this purpose by the good Fr. Eudes, expressed himself this way: "The adorable Heart of Our Lord being a furnace of love towards His Father and of charity towards us, and the source of an infinity of graces and favors for the entire human race, all men, especially all Christians, have infinite obligations to honor, praise, and glorify it in every possible way."

That same year, another French bishop, the Bishop of Coutances, said in turn: "The adorable Heart of our Redeemer being the first object of the holy love and delight of the Father of mercies, and being reciprocally all enveloped with holy love towards this God of consolation as also being all inflamed with charity towards us, all burning with zeal for our salvation, all full of mercy towards sinners, all full of compassion towards the destitute, and the principle of all the glories and happiness of heaven, of all graces and earthly blessings, and an inexhaustible source of all kinds of favors for those who honor it, all Christians must strive to render it all the veneration and adoration possible."

Nothing is more certain than this doctrine. Note in fact:

The Holy Ghost is Love itself; He is eternal, substantial, and living Love. Now, He reposes in fullness in the holy soul of Jesus—He is like the light which is fully condensed within the sun, which from there pours out over the world. But the soul of the Son of God loving but by means of the Heart with which it is united, it follows that the Sacred Heart of Jesus is the visible hearth of divine love in the middle of the world. It is, as St. Bernardine of Siena admirably says, "a furnace of most ardent charity, to inflame and set the world on fire."[1] And the fire of this furnace is the Holy Ghost, it is eternal Love.

The Spirit of love reposes and lives in the Heart of Jesus Christ, like a dove in its nest. He burns in this Divine Heart, like fire in the coal that it enflames, and it is from here, from this ineffable Heart, that He propagates into the heart of anyone who is capable of loving.

The Heart of Jesus is firstly the hearth of the love of God. Our Lord loves His Father with an absolutely divine love, since He is Himself God, as is His Father, and since He loves God with the soul and the heart of a God. The entirety of this bottomless, limitless ocean of love passes through the Heart of the Son of Mary, and from there it loses itself eternally in the bosom of the Father. Like an irresistible torrent, it first amasses, and then it pulls in after it all creatures, angels and men, who want to love the good God. All the love of God that makes palpitate the heart of the Blessed Virgin, and the heart of the seraphim, cherubim, archangels, and angels; all the love that sanctified the patriarchs, prophets, saints, and faithful of the Old Testament; all the love of the apostles, martyrs, and faithful of the Law of Grace; all this love emanates from the Sacred Heart of Jesus, like an inexhaustible,

---

[1] Fornax ardentissimæ charitatis, ad inflammandum et incendendum orbem terrarum (Serm. de Passio. Dni, part. II, tit. 1).

infinite source. In the world of souls, the Heart of Jesus Christ is the sun of the love of God.

O my Savior, I give myself to You to unite myself with the eternal, immense, and infinite love You bear Your Father. O adorable Father, through the Incarnation, through grace, and through the Eucharist, You have given me Your beloved Son; He is mine, His Sacred Heart is mine. I therefore offer You all the eternal, immense, and infinite love of Your Son Jesus, as a love that is mine. And in this way, just as Jesus tells us, *"As the Father hath loved Me, I also have loved you"* (Jn 15:9), I can likewise say to You, I too, O my divine Father, "As Your Son loves You, I also love You."

Oh, what a grace to be members of Jesus Christ, and to be able in this way to love through His Heart, to love with His Heart!

The divine Heart of Jesus is also the source of the love of the Blessed Virgin. After His heavenly Father, Our Lord loves nothing as much as His Holy Mother; or rather, as a true son, He loves her with the same love with which He loves His Father, never separating them in His divine tenderness. Here again, it is through His Heart and it is by means of His Heart that the Incarnate Word loves the Most Blessed Virgin; and He communicates this filial love to all hearts who allow Him to do so. The love that we bear for the Virgin Mary, the love with which we will love her for all eternity, springs from its source, from the Heart of Jesus Christ.

And it is likewise for all pure and legitimate love, in heaven and on earth; it comes from the single Source, from the living Source of love; it comes from, it springs from the most loving and most adorable Heart of Jesus

Christ. Very often, alas, we abuse this treasure, and the love that we give our God, we divert it from its true object; however, in itself, this love nonetheless remains a most pure gift, and to profane it is a true sacrilege.

Thus, the Heart that beat on the earth long ago, which beats eternally in heaven in the sacred chest of Jesus, is the adorable and adored hearth of the love of God and love of creatures. Oh, how much we must love it! How much we must lovingly throw ourselves and lose ourselves in this abyss of love!

Yet, O Savior, I am poor and miserable, and I am unable, as needed, to cast my heart into Your Heart. Do a little for me, merciful Jesus, what you did for your blessed servant in the Visitation: deign to take my weak heart and immerse it, like the heart of Sister Margaret Mary, into Your Heart all burning with love. Inflame it, melt the ice of its natural selfishness, and only return it to me as a flame of love, which will thenceforth make me love everything, like You and in You.

XI

How the Most Holy Trinity is living and reigning in the Heart of Jesus

Here is a truly divine proof of the ineffable excellence of the Sacred Heart: it is the living sanctuary of the Most Holy Trinity, which lives and reigns in it, in all fullness.

The eternal Father is in this admirable Heart as in the Heart of His beloved Son, in Whom He is well pleased.

The Father eternally begets His Son; He eternally communicates to Him His eternal life. He lives and reigns in Him in time, in His holy humanity, with this same all-divine life He gives Him in eternity. The Heart of Jesus is in effect, by reason of the hypostatic union, the very Heart of the eternal Son of the Father. What infinite grandeur! How much the heavenly Father must love the divine Heart of Jesus!

O good Jesus, engrave the image Yourself of Your most meek and most humble Heart in our poor hearts. Make them also to live only on love for Your heavenly Father, Who, through You and in You, has become our true Father.

The Eternal Word lives and reigns in this royal Heart, which He has united to Himself in the most intimate union that can be conceived, namely, the hypostatic union. By virtue of this union, this Heart, this Heart of flesh, this created Heart, is the true Heart of the Eternal Word; and it is adorable with the same adoration which is due to the Word, which is adoration due to God.

What a reign is the reign of the Son of God in His Sacred Heart! In man, the heart is the principle of life, the seat of love, of hatred, of joy, of sadness, of anger, of fear, and of all the other passions of the soul. In the Heart of Jesus Christ, these passions did not have, it is true, the disordered character that they have in us, since they were all absolutely and always subject to His most holy will; but they existed there in fullness, and they were wondrously subject to the divine will of the Eternal Word. What a beautiful reign!

O Jesus, are you not rightfully the King of my heart? Live in it, and thereby reign over my passions. Alas, they are not in me, as in You, subject to Your holy will. Unite them to Your most perfect passions, and do not permit that they ever act independently of Your governance or for any purpose but Your glory alone.

The third person of the august Trinity, the Holy Spirit, inseparable from the Son and the Father, also lives and reigns in the Heart of Jesus in an ineffable manner. This Spirit of love concentrates there the infinite treasures of the knowledge and wisdom of God; He fills it with all His gifts in a sovereign degree, according to these divine words of Scripture: *"And the Spirit of the Lord shall rest upon Him: the Spirit of wisdom and of understanding, the Spirit of counsel and of fortitude, the Spirit of knowledge and of godliness. And He shall be filled with the Spirit of the fear of the Lord"* (Is 11:2-3). The Holy Spirit fecundates the Heart of Jesus, and has it produce, like a divine earth, the so delicious, so sweet fruits the Apostle St. Paul enumerates: *"The fruit of the Spirit is charity, joy, peace, patience, benignity, goodness, longanimity, mildness, faith, modesty, continency, chastity"* (Gal 5:22-23).

Inseparable from each other and being but one single God, the three divine persons thus live and reign together in the Heart of the Savior, as in the most sublime throne of their love, in the first heaven of their glory, in the Paradise of their dearest delights. They spread there, so to speak, over and over, with a superabundance and incredible profuseness, incomprehensible lights, immense oceans of graces, torrents of fires and infinitely burning flames, and all the effusions of their eternal love.

O Most Holy Trinity, my God, infinite praises be rendered to You forever for all the miracles of love You work in the Heart of my beloved Jesus. I offer You my heart, with those of all my brethren, most humbly imploring You to fully take possession of them, to destroy everything in them that displeases You, and to sovereignly establish there the reign of Your divine love.

O Most Holy Trinity, eternal life of hearts, reign in my heart forever.

XII

That the Heart of Jesus is the Temple, Altar, and Censer of divine love

It was uncreated and eternal Love, meaning the Holy Ghost, Who erected this magnificent *Temple*, and Who formed it from the virginal blood of the Mother of love.

This living Temple was consecrated and sanctified by the "*High Priest, holy, innocent, undefiled... and made higher than the heavens*" (Heb 7:26), by the "*great High Priest that hath passed into the heavens, Jesus the Son of God*" (Heb 4:14). It was consecrated by the unction of divinity. It is dedicated to eternal Love. It is infinitely more holy, more worthy, and more venerable than all material and spiritual temples which have been and will ever be in heaven and on earth.

It is in this Heart, in this august Temple, that God receives adoration, praise, and glory worthy of His infinite grandeur. It is in this Temple that the Supreme Preacher, Who is the Word, meaning the word of God in person, continuously preaches to us. It is in this heavenly Temple holier than the heavens that the Eternal Priest offers to the divine majesty, in the name of all creation, the sacrifice of eternal adoration, eternal thanksgiving, and eternal love.

It is the sanctuary, the center of holiness, which does not know profanation. It is adorned with all the evangelical virtues and all the perfections of the divine essence, as so many rich sculptures and living paintings. O holy humanity of Jesus! O deified Heart, glorious center of this thrice holy humanity!

Be blessed, my God, for having erected for Yourself this wondrous Temple, and for having deigned to grant me access to it! I dare to unite myself to Your Jesus and my Jesus, to render You, in the Temple of His Heart, the adoration, the thanksgiving, and all the other homage due to Your sovereign majesty.

But the Heart of Jesus is not only the Temple, it is also the *Altar* of divine love.

It is on this Altar of pure gold that the sacred fire of this same love is lit day and night. It is on this same Altar that the Sovereign Priest Jesus continuously offers all kinds of sacrifices to the Most Holy Trinity. He firstly offers Himself and sacrifices Himself as a victim of love, as the most holy and most precious victim that ever was and can be. He entirely sacrifices His soul, His body, His blood, and His life, with all His thoughts, all His words, all His actions, and everything He suffered on earth. And this sacrifice, He offers it perpetually on the living altar of His Heart; He offers it with an immense, infinite love.

Secondly, He offers as a sacrifice of adoration and praise all that His Father has given Him, meaning heaven and earth, angels, men, and all animate and inanimate creatures; He offers them to the divine majesty as so many victims destined to render glory to God.

He even offers and sacrifices to the holiness of God the rebellious creatures who, through sin, evade love: bad

Christians, the impious, heretics, the reprobate, and the demons themselves. He sacrifices through the sword of divine justice all those who elude the sweet and free immolation of love. Nothing escapes Him: the damned no more than the elect, the demons no more than the angels, and hell no more than earth and heaven.

It is in this way that Jesus Christ, the eternal Priest according to the order of Melchisedech, offers Himself and offers all things with an absolutely divine joy[1] to the glory of His Father, on the Altar of the Sacred Heart, the most lovable and at the same time the most redoubtable of altars.

O Jesus! Jesus, my love! Jesus, my mercy and my good Master! Place me, all unworthy that I am, among the number of the victims of Your love. Consume me entirely, like a holocaust of this love, in the divine fires that incessantly burn on the sacred Altar of Your Heart.

Lastly, the Sacred Heart of Jesus is also the *Censer* of divine love.

It is this golden Censer that is spoken of in the eighth chapter of the Apocalypse, and which St. Augustine interprets as the adorable Heart of Jesus. *"And another angel came, and stood before the altar, having a golden censer; and there was given to him much incense, that he should offer of the prayers of all saints upon the golden altar, which is before the throne of God"* (Rv 8:3). All these words are full of Jesus: this Angel offering to God's majesty the incense of the prayers of the Saints in His censer is Jesus, the Angel of the new and everlasting Covenant, Who offers to His Father the prayers of all His faithful, uniting them to His divine prayer. The censer of

---

[1] Laetus obtuli universa (1 Chr 29:17).

pure gold is again Jesus, it is the Heart of Jesus: the burning coals of love fill this Sacred Heart, and, lighting the incense of the prayer of the Saints, make it to rise, like a fragrant vapor, to the throne of God. This golden altar, of which we just spoke, is Jesus, still Jesus. Finally, the throne of God, it is again Our Lord, Whose holy humanity is the true throne where God's majesty resides.

In the Censer of the most holy Heart of Jesus are placed, to be offered to God and to be sanctified and deified, all the adoration, praise, petitions, prayers, affections, and aspirations of all the Saints and Angels. Let us take care to faithfully respond to this design of Providence by placing in our heavenly Censer all our prayers, desires, devotion, and pious affections of our hearts. Let us place our very hearts there, with all that we do and all that we are, beseeching the King of hearts to purify and sanctify all these things, and then to offer them to His Father as a most pure incense, in an odor of sweetness.[1]

Yes, the Sacred Heart of our Jesus is the Temple, the Altar, and the Censer at the same time as the Priest and the Victim of divine love. And it is all of this for us! And it is for us, who are poor and miserable, that it exercises these divine functions!

O love! O excess of love! O my Savior, how Your goodness is admirable towards me. Oh, what veneration and what praise am I not obliged to render to Your Sacred Heart!

O most sweet Heart of my Jesus, may I be all heart and all love for You, and may all the hearts of heaven and earth be immolated to Your praise and to Your glory!

---

[1] Offerre illi incensum dignum, in odorem suavitatis (Sir 45).

XIII

How the Heart of Jesus is the life principle of the Man-God, the Mother of God, and the children of God

Here is another reason to admire and adore most profoundly the Heart of Our Lord Jesus Christ: it is the principle of His life, and consequently the principle of the life of His Mother and of all His faithful.

Jesus is life. He said so Himself: "*I am the Life; ego sum Vita*" (Jn 11 and 14). His Heart, which is the most excellent part of Himself, is thus what is most excellent and most living in Him Who is Life. This divine Heart can be contemplated with respect to the body of Jesus and with respect to His soul. For one as for the other, it is the life principle.

It is the life principle of the body of Our Lord, because it is from it, as a life-giving source, that it spreads into all the members, into all the parts of the Savior's body, the divine blood that is the life of this adorable body. The Holy Ghost says so in fact: "*The life... is in the blood*" (Lv 17:11, 14). The warmth of life resides entirely in the blood, and the blood comes from the heart.

The spiritual Heart of Jesus, meaning His most holy soul united to His heart of flesh and contemplated in what of it is the most sublime, the intellect and love, is equally the seat and principle of the life of Jesus's soul. It is in fact in this spiritual Heart, in this superior and intimate part of the soul of Jesus Christ, that the hypostatic union is effected, which unites the divinity and humanity of the Son of God so much that one and the other, from now on inseparable, together form the one and indivisible person of our Savior. From this deified Heart all the torrents of divine light and divine love spread into the soul of Jesus.

The Sacred Heart is therefore in Jesus the principle of His life: all the thoughts and affections that the Son of God had in this world for our salvation, all the words that He said, all the actions that He did, all the sufferings that He deigned to endure, the incomprehensible holiness and love with which He did and suffered all these things, in a word everything in Him proceeded and flowed from His divine Heart, like streams from their source.

It is therefore to the Sacred Heart that we are indebted; it is from it, it is from the Heart of Jesus that flows our salvation. What shall we do to give You thanks, O good Jesus? We shall offer You this adorable Heart which You deigned to make our own. Yes, I offer it with confidence, in union with the infinite love that inspired it to work such admirable things for my redemption.

The Heart of Jesus is secondly the principle of life of the Mother of God; for, just as the virginal heart of this admirable Mother was the principle of the bodily and natural life of her Child whilst she carried Him in her chaste womb, the Heart of this adorable Child was in turn the principle of the spiritual and supernatural life of His most holy Mother. The deified Heart of the Son of Mary was thus the principle of all the pious thoughts and affections of His Blessed Mother, of all the holy words that she spoke, of all the good actions that she did, of all the virtues that she practiced, and of the wondrous holiness with which she suffered so many pains and so many sorrows in cooperating with her Son in the work of our salvation.

Eternal praises, O my Jesus, be rendered to Your divine Heart! O my Redeemer, in thanksgiving for what the Blessed Virgin, Your Mother and our Mother, deigned to do for us, I offer You what You love most in the world, after Your Father: the Immaculate Heart of Your Mother, all ablaze with love for You.

Thirdly, the Heart of Jesus is the principle of the spiritual and supernatural life of all the children of God. This supernatural life is like an expansion and a blossoming of the all-divine life that Jesus communicates to His Mother.

Since the Heart of Jesus is the life principle of the Head, it is also the life principle of the members. And since it is the life principle of the Mother, it is thereby the life principle of the children.

Similar to that mysterious fountain that gushes forth from the middle of the earthly paradise to flow over all the earth to make it fertile, the Heart of Jesus is, in the middle of the Church, as the universal source of holiness. It is from this source that rush forth the living waters of the Holy Ghost, the waters that gush up in us unto eternal life.

The Heart of Jesus is the principle and origin of all the good thoughts which have ever been or ever will be, until the end of time and into eternity, in the minds of all Christians, the principle and origin of all the holy words which have come out of or will come out of their mouths, of all the actions of piety which have proceeded or will proceed from their hands, of all the virtues that they have practiced or will practice, and finally, of all the merits they have acquired or will be able to acquire in working, suffering, and dying for Jesus Christ.

O my Savior, may all these things be converted into eternal praise to Your Most Holy Heart! O Jesus, since You have given me this same Heart to be the principle of my life, please make it to be the sole principle of all my sentiments and all my affections; that through its most ardent charity it vivify and move, as through a mystical blood, all the powers of my soul, in such a way that it no longer be I, but it and it alone, that lives in me.

Finally, make it to be the soul of my soul, the mind of my mind, and the heart of my heart.

O Heart of Jesus Christ, principle of all good, glory to You, in heaven and on earth, in time and in eternity!

XIV

That the adorable Heart of Jesus is a furnace of love with regard to the Most Blessed Virgin Mary

We have indicated it already, but we must return to and emphasize it: after His heavenly Father, Jesus did not and does not love anything as much as His most good, most holy, and most sweet Mother.

The ineffable graces with which the Son of God filled His Blessed Mother clearly show that He has for her a love without measure and without limit. He loves her, her alone, incomparably more than all His Angels and all His Saints, more than all His other creatures together.

Firstly, this Blessed Virgin is *the sole one*[1] whom the Son of God chose from all eternity to raise her above all

---

[1] Una est columba mea (Sg 6:8).

creation, to set her on the most sublime throne of glory and grandeur, and to confer on her the most prodigious of all dignities, the dignity of Mother of God.

If we look at "the fullness of time" from the perspective of eternity, we see that this Most Holy Virgin is the only one among the children of Adam whom, by an entirely special privilege, God preserved from original sin. He thus made her all beautiful, all pure, and all immaculate, setting her to crush the head of Satan.

And not only did the love of God preserve her from original sin, but moreover, from the first moment of her immaculate conception, He filled her with such preeminent grace that she surpassed the grace of the first of the Seraphim, the grace of innocent Adam, and the grace of the greatest of all the Saints. And as a result of this unique privilege, the Most Blessed Virgin makes, at the very moment she begins to live, an act of adoration and love more perfect than that of the most ardent of Seraphim.

In His filial love, Our Lord yet gave to her, and gave to her alone, to love and adore her God perfectly, continuously, and without any interruption during the entire course of her life. Thus, one can say that from the first moment of her life until the last, she made but a single act of love.

To her alone was it given to accomplish in fullness the first of the divine commandments: *You will adore and love the Lord your God with all your heart, all your strength, and all your soul.*[1]

---

[1] Dominum Deum tuum adorabis (Mt 4:10; Lk 4:8). Diliges Dominum Deum tuum ex toto corde tuo, ex tota anima tua, et ex tota fortitudine tua (Dt 6:5; Mt 22:37; Mk 12:30; Lk 10:27).

To her alone was it given to engender from her own substance Him Who from all eternity is begotten from the substance of the Father. She gave a part of her virginal substance and of her most pure blood to form the holy humanity of the Son of God; and much more, she cooperated, and cooperated freely, with the Father, the Son, and the Holy Ghost, in the union of her substance with the adorable person of the Son of God; and she thereby cooperated in the accomplishment of the mystery of the Incarnation, that is to say the greatest miracle that God has ever done, will ever do, and even ever could do. What a privilege! What a glory for this Most Holy Virgin!

That is not all. The most pure blood and the virginal flesh that the Virgin Mary gave to Jesus in this ineffable mystery of love will remain united for eternity, through the hypostatic union, to the person of the Incarnate Word, which is why in the humanity of the Son of God, this virginal blood and this precious flesh from Mary are *adorable*, adorable in the very adoration that is due to this humanity; and they indeed are and will forever be the object of the adoration of all the Angels and all the Saints. Here below, whilst awaiting heaven, we adore them beneath the veils of the Eucharist. O love of Jesus towards Mary!

She alone, this admirable Mother, provided the substance with which was formed the Sacred Heart of the Child Jesus; and it was from her substance that, for nine months, this Divine Heart took its nourishment and development. It is from Mary that we have the Sacred Heart.

She alone is simultaneously Mother and Virgin; she alone bore in her chaste womb for nine months Him

Whom the Eternal Father bears in His bosom for all eternity; she alone, the sweet Virgin Mary, nursed and made live Him Who is Eternal Life and Who gives life to everything that is living. Milk is like the flower and essence of the mother's blood—Mary gave her milk to the Child-God and had Him repose on her breast like a delightful daybed. She alone, true Mother of Him Who is true God, saw herself obeyed by the sovereign monarch of the universe, something which honors her infinitely more than could possibly do all the homage of beings created or that God could ever create.

She alone, and St. Joseph at her side, remained continuously with this adorable Savior during the thirty-three years He spent on earth. An amazing thing! The Son of God came down to save all men, and yet, to preach to them and instruct them, He gave them only three years and three months of His life, whereas He consecrated more than thirty years to His holy Mother to ever sanctify her more and more.

Oh, what torrents of graces and blessings He incessantly poured, during all that time, into the soul of His beloved Mother, who was so well-disposed to receive them! Oh, with what heavenly fires and flames the divine Heart of Jesus, a furnace of most ardent charity, ever more and more inflamed the Immaculate Heart of His most sweet Mother, especially when these two Hearts were so close to each other and so intimately united, first when she carried Him in her chaste womb, and later when she fed Him with her milk and she carried Him in her arms and on her holy breast, and during all the time she lived with Him in Nazareth, that she lived familiarly with Him as a mother with her child, that she drank and ate with

Him, that she prayed with Him and that she heard the words coming from His adored mouth, similar to so many burning coals ever more and more inflaming her most holy Heart with the sacred fire of divine love.

To make better understood, if needed, the immensity of the love of Jesus for His Mother, let us further state that only she was transported body and soul into heaven, and that she was elevated there above all the choirs of Angels and Saints, to the right hand of her Son; that she alone is crowned Queen of angels and men, Sovereigness of heaven and earth; that she alone has all power over the Church triumphant, militant, and suffering;[1] that finally, she alone has more merit before her Son Jesus than all the inhabitants of heaven together,[2] because in heaven she preserves with her status as Mother of God the authority that this august title conferred her over the Heart of Jesus Christ. In heaven, she is, as St. Bernard admirably says, the all-powerful suppliant, *"omnipotentia supplex."*

What prodigies of grace the Heart of our Savior has thus amassed in His holy Mother! What obliged Him to do this, if not the most ardent love with which His filial Heart is inflamed in her regard?

And He loves her so much because she is His Mother. He loves her more, her alone, than all creatures together, because she has more love for Him than all the angels and all the elect of heaven and earth. He loves her so ardently because she cooperated with Him in His great work, which is the work of the world's redemption and sanctification.

---

[1] In Jerusalem potestas mea (Sir 24:15).
[2] Data est tibi omnis potestas in cœlo et in terra (St. Peter Damian).

O adorable Heart of the only son of Mary, my heart is full of joy in seeing that You have so much love for Your most sweet Mother! O Jesus, Son of God and of Mary, inflame my heart with the love You bear for Your Mother! You said to us, *"I have given you an example, that as I have done... so you do also"* (Jn 13:15). You thereby order me to love as much as I can her whom You love so much. O Mother of love, yes, I love you with all my heart, with your Jesus, Who is also my Jesus.

Let us all love her, this most holy Mother; let us love her like Jesus does, let us love her with Jesus and in Jesus! And let us from now on have but one heart with Jesus and Mary: a heart which detests what they detest, that is to say sin in all its forms; a heart which loves what they love, especially innocence, humility, and abnegation.

O Mother of goodness, obtain for us this grace from your Son's so loving Heart!

XV

What the Heart of Jesus was for His holy Mother during His Passion

Jesus being the most perfect and best son there ever was, He felt with most bitter sorrow the impact from the terrible sorrows His beloved Mother had to suffer during all His life, but principally in the days of His Passion. The sorrows of Jesus were those of Mary, and the sorrows of Mary were those of Jesus.

The day of this sorrowful Passion having arrived, Our Lord, obeying until death His holy Mother as much as His heavenly Father, asked the Most Blessed Virgin, the saints say, to acquiesce to His bloody sacrifice, which she did with a love and a sorrow impossible to imagine. Jesus made known to her what He had to suffer, and asked her to accompany Him in spirit and body in His sufferings.

Mary therefore offered her Heart and Jesus delivered His body; and in this way the Mother had to suffer in her Heart all the torments of her Son, and the Son had to suffer all together the inconceivable tortures in His body, and in His Sacred Heart those of the Heart of His mother.

The Savior, having taken leave from His beloved Mother, then went to immerse Himself in the immense ocean of His sorrows, carrying like a sharp arrow piercing His Heart the thought and desolations of her whom He loved above all. For her part, the Blessed Virgin, entering into a profound prayer, began to accompany Him interiorly, and to share with Him the anguish of His agony. She said with Him: *Lord, not my will, but Yours be done; non mea voluntas, sed tua fiat!* (Lk 22:42).

During the terrible night of the Passion, the Blessed Virgin followed in spirit her dear adorable Jesus, betrayed, abandoned, struck, covered with insults and outrages, buffeted, and spat upon. What a night! The Heart of Jesus did not leave for an instant the torn Heart of His Mother, and unceasingly sent her extraordinary graces so that she could suffer everything without dying. Among other graces, He sent her the good and beloved St. John, who no longer left her, and whom she led, alone among all the Apostles, up to the foot of the Cross and to the sepulchre.

Knowing the moment was approaching when she was to follow, not only in heart but in body, the divine Victim up to the bloody altar of sacrifice, she went out at daybreak accompanied by St. John, St. Mary Magdalene, and the other holy women. Soon, mixed in the crowd of people, she caught sight of her Son, her Lord, her God, her one love; she saw Him pale and disfigured, being dragged like a vile criminal from the palace of Caiphas to the palace of Pilate; resent from the palace of Pilate to that of Herod, from where He was again sent back to Pilate, covered in the cloak of a madman, and holding in His hand the derisive reed scepter. She saw Him, her meek and innocent Lamb, scourged and blood-soaked in the praetorium; then, crowned with thorns and shown to the people. She heard Him being condemned to death. In her ears, the murderous crowd hurled the horrible blasphemy: *"Crucify him, crucify him!... We have no king but Caesar"* (Jn 19:6, 15).

And during all this time, Jesus was looking at His Mother, sometimes with the eyes of the body, always with the eyes of the Heart! What anguish in this gaze! Imitating her Lamb, Who was letting Himself be immolated in silence, Mary, like the Ewe of God, was weeping and suffering in silence. Silence alone could suit such sorrows.

The mournful procession set off. The Ewe could follow her Lamb in the very trail of His blood. She mixed this divine blood with the blood of her Heart, that is her tears. She saw her Beloved, her Jesus, fall underneath the weight of the Cross. She saw Him climb the slope of Calvary. She saw Him, nailed on the terrible Cross, go up, like a bloody standard of salvation and hope, of love and justice, of life and death, and dominate the multitude. Love obliged her to draw as near as possible to her adorable Son; and during those long hours she suffered with Jesus sorrows that man will never be able to comprehend, divine sorrows, as St. Bonaventure says. What Jesus hanging on the Cross suffered in His soul and in His body, this is what the Mother of sorrows suffered in her Heart.

And from the height of the Cross, through the tears and the blood obscuring His eyes, the Redeemer contemplated His most holy Mother, and gave to her sufferings an infinite merit. The most sacred Ewe and the divine Lamb looked at each other without saying anything; they communicated their sorrows to each other. And as the sacrifice advanced towards its end, as the holy Victim entered the throes of the final agony, the unspeakable suffering of Jesus and consequently of Mary, of Mary and consequently of Jesus, rose, ever rose, like water at high tide. It arrived at its fullness when, everything being consummated, the crucified Eternal Word let out His last cry of horrible anguish and of triumph, lowered His head, and gave up His spirit. Jesus expired while looking at His Mother. She was the first one to receive this divine gaze, in Bethlehem, at the moment when the Son of God came into the world; it was fitting that she be the last one to enjoy this gaze, at the moment when the mystery of Redemption was completed on Golgotha.

Oh, what mysteries of sorrow and love in that last look of Jesus expiring! It fell onto the purest and most immaculate of creatures, onto the Virgin without stain, onto the sacred Spouse of the Eternal Father, onto the Mother of God, onto the masterpiece of the Holy Ghost. It fell onto the best of all mothers, onto her whom Jesus cherished more, her alone, than all the creatures of earth and heaven; onto the most faithful companion of His entire life, of all His works.

It was the Heart of Jesus crucified which, from the height of the Cross, gave to us all, and to each one, in the person of the faithful St. John, the Most Blessed Virgin to be our Mother. Yes, it was from the depths of this Heart full of love that came those two utterances inscribed in letters of fire in the hearts of all true Christians: "Behold your son!" and *"Behold your Mother!"* Receiving as Mother the immaculate Mother of God, what a bequest! What a present! What a divine gift! One indeed recognizes in this the Sacred Heart of Jesus, it alone being capable of such an excess of tenderness! And it is by giving them Mary, that it avenges itself on sinners!

Good Jesus, most innocent Lamb Who in Your Passion suffered so much, and Who saw the virginal heart of Your Mother immersed in an ocean of sorrows, please teach me to accompany You, like her, in Your afflictions.

Teach me to hate sin. Teach me to be a good son to Your Mother. O my poor heart, so weak and so guilty, will you not melt in sorrow in seeing that you are the cause of the indescribable sorrows of this holy Mother and of this most sweet Savior?

O Jesus crucified, the love of my heart! O Mary, my consolation and my Mother! Imprint in my soul a great contempt for the vanities and pleasures of this world, and make me to ever keep before my eyes Your sacred sorrows, to which I owe my salvation and my eternal happiness.

XVI

That the adorable Heart of Jesus is a furnace of love with regard to the Church triumphant, the Church militant, and the Church suffering

The Sacred Heart of Jesus is the hearth from which emanate all the light and ardor filling with purity, beauty, beatitude, and love the Church in heaven, the Church on earth, and the Church in purgatory. The all-powerful flames of this divine Heart set even hell on fire, with the demons and the reprobate; but these are only avenging flames of scorned love, the "eternal ardors" of eternal love which envelop in the redoubtable holiness of justice all those who have rejected the sweet holiness of love.

The Sacred Heart therefore penetrates, illuminates, and beatifies the Church in heaven. Let us go up in thought to the blessed Paradise, where Jesus prepares us our place. What is this infinite number of angels, saints, patriarchs, prophets, apostles, martyrs, confessors, virgins, and blessed of every age, condition, and nation? What is this, if not so many ardent flames from the immense furnace of the Heart of the Holy of Holies?

Is this not goodness and love, is this not the grace of this divine Heart which created them all, which enlightened them with the light of faith, which made them Christians, which gave them the strength to overcome the demon, the world, and the flesh, which adorned them with all the virtues, which sanctified them in this world, which has glorified them in the next, which has kindled in their faithful hearts the love they bear for God, which has filled their mouths with His divine praises, and which is the source of everything that is great, holy, and admirable in them? If, then, we celebrate in the course of the year so many beautiful feast days in honor of these same saints, if we render them such a solemn and at the same time such a legitimate veneration, what will we not do to honor, celebrate, and glorify the divine Heart that is the principle of the holiness of all the saints and of the beatitude of all the blessed!

The Heart of Jesus is the Heart of Paradise and the sun of glory of this beautiful living heaven where, by His mercy, we hope to arrive one day.

If from the Church in heaven we come back to the Church on earth, we see here again the marvels of the Heart and love of Jesus Christ. It is the heart and life of the world of grace, like it is the heart and life of the world of glory.

Is it not the love of Jesus which, in constituting His Church militant, has safeguarded the faith of Christians by means of the infallible papacy and of the holy hierarchy of pastors? Is it not He Who instituted the priesthood and sends us our priests, that is our saviors, our directors, our guardians, our spiritual fathers, and our true consolers? If we have genuine faith, if we are Christians, to what do we owe this, if not to the love, to the Sacred Heart of Jesus Christ?

It is He, He alone, Who in the sacraments of the Church has exhausted, so to speak, all the wonders and all the inventions of infinite mercy. What a treasure of love is Baptism, where Jesus, applying to us the fullness of His merits of His sacrifice, purifies and sanctifies us so gratuitously, that when receiving this great sacrament, we did not even know what we were receiving! Who is the man who would have been capable of finding in his own heart such a thought?

What a treasure of mercy is this ineffable sacrament of Penance, in which divine love, without sacrificing anything of its infinite holiness, goes much further yet than in Baptism, extends pardon with a dazzling profusion, and forgives everything, always forgiving the truly repentant! O adorably good Heart of my Savior! O truly divine mercy!

What a treasure, what a treasure of love is this Eucharist, called for this reason "the sacrament of love"! Here, heaven unites with earth; here, beneath this veil of snow, truly and bodily resides on our altars the King of Angels and of Saints, the good Jesus, the Heart of Jesus. He is in our midst, day and night, without care for His own glory, seeking only our heart and our happiness. There is no mother who could forget herself as much for her child. And yet, what is the heart of a mother, if not synonymous with tenderness, love, and devotion? The Heart of Jesus is indeed more than that for His dear Church.

And what to say of the other sacraments? What to say of the Gospel? Of Scripture? Of the thousand and one institutions of charity and mercy which are the crown of the Holy Church throughout the earth? What to say of holy indulgences and all other treasures of grace?

All of that, yes, all of that is but the radiance of the love of the Sacred Heart of Jesus. O Lord, what an inestimable grace to be born and to live in the bosom of Your Church! It is indeed, truly, to be born and to live in Your divine Heart, in the bosom of Your love.

Finally, the Church suffering in purgatory is also filled with the sacred flames of the Heart of Jesus. It is true, it is the holiness of justice that dominates there; but love also has a large part there. For if there were no purgatory, heaven would remain shut to most men. Indeed, is it not a truth of faith that into the kingdom of heaven *"there shall not enter... anything defiled"* (Rv 21:27)? And is it not also certain that, even among the most faithful of the faithful, there is almost no one who lives a sufficiently pure life and does sufficiently perfect penance to be able, at the moment of death, to enter immediately and directly into heaven? Thus, the Church in purgatory entirely owes its existence, its salvation, and its unshakeable and eternal hopes to the merciful Heart of Jesus.

Moreover, it is from this most good Heart that come all the consolations that temper the expiations of the faithful in purgatory. It is He, it is Jesus, Who sends them His Holy Mother as a consolatrix, and Who incessantly stirs the hearts of the faithful on earth with such charitable and burning zeal to first relieve and then deliver these poor souls, by means of the Mass, communion, indulgences, alms, and all good Catholic works.

Such, then, is the infinite love of Our Lord for His Church, whether in heaven, on earth, or in purgatory. Such is His adorable Heart, from which depart and return, to rest there eternally, all the creatures who have the happiness of knowing the true God, of adoring, loving, and serving Him.

XVII

That the Divine Heart of Jesus is also a furnace of love with regard to each one of us

What Our Lord is for all His faithful in general and what He has done for all, He is so and does so for each of them individually. Each one of us is, so to speak, Jesus's abridged world, the abridgement of His Church, and the abridgement of His natural and supernatural creation.

I can sum up in two statements what the Son of God did for me as well as for each of us individually: He withdraws me from an abyss of evils, and He opens before my faithfulness a world of goods and happiness.

Original sin had me born into a supernatural state of degradation and death, the horror of which my mind cannot conceive. I was a *"child of wrath,"* according to the redoubtable expression of Scripture (Eph 2:3). I was the enemy of my God and the object of His malediction. I was excommunicated from the Most Holy Trinity, anathematized by the Father, the Son, and the Holy Ghost, separated from the company of the angels, banished from the house of my heavenly Father, excluded from heaven, destined for hell, condemned to the devouring flames of eternal fire, subject to Satan's horrible tyranny; and this forever, without hope of any help. I was irremediably lost.

I was in *sin*, meaning in the evil of evils, the sole cause of all the evils that desolate the earth and hell in time and in eternity. Oh, what an abyss is sin! Without being infinite in the creature who commits it and who is not capable of the infinite, it is however in itself a truly infinite evil, because it violates the holiness of God, Who is infinite, because it offends an infinite majesty, goodness, power, and wisdom; and this is why in strict justice it deserves an infinite penalty, at least as concerns its duration.

To expiate it worthily and fully requires a victim of infinite worth, in other words a divine victim. Even if all the angels, all the seraphim and virtues of heaven were to become incarnate and suffer and die; even if all the saints from the beginning until the end of the world were to jointly offer their such magnificent merits, their prayers, penances, tears, and holy works; even if all were to shed their blood to the last drop; even if, oh marvel, the most holy and immaculate Virgin Mary were to offer God the ineffable merits of her life and death, the abyss of sin would yet remain wide open, its infinite aspect unable to be filled through the efforts of any creature. Indeed, the abyss of sin is nothing other than the abyss of hell.

Thus, if my most merciful, most good, and thousand times blessed Savior had not become man to come and save me; if He had not wept and suffered for miserable me; if His divine sacrifice had not redeemed my death, my eternal death, no creature in heaven or on earth could have withdrawn me from the abyss of sin and delivered me from death and anathema, nor even refreshed me by means of that drop of water that the evil rich man (who is nothing but a sinner) has so long asked for in vain.

However, by incomprehensible good fortune, I see myself taken from this abyss of woe. To whom do I owe this, to whom? O Jesus, You know: it is to You alone! Yes, it is Your infinite love, it is Your Sacred Heart, the organ and hearth of this love; it is the immense goodness, infinite mercy, and incomparable love of Your Heart that have saved me! The sacred flames of Your Heart have returned life to me and extinguished the flames of my frightful hell.

And this You did gratuitously, and more than gratuitously since I was not only void of merits before You, but an all-defiled reprobate, horrible and infected. What a grace, my God! What a mystery of love!

And what Jesus Christ did for me by admitting me to Baptism, He renews it superabundantly a thousand and a thousand times; He renews it incessantly in the sacrament of Penance, always forgiving me; yes, always, always; forgiving me everything; never tiring. He only knows how to avenge Himself by forgiving.

This is what the Heart of my Jesus has done for me.

"What shall I render to the Lord, for all the things He hath rendered unto me? I will take the chalice of salvation" (Ps 115:12-13) and I will offer to my heavenly Benefactor a thanksgiving worthy of Him. One day St. Teresa, praying before the Blessed Sacrament, found herself as though crushed beneath the weight of the divine mercies, and she felt a great anguish in being unable to be thankful for them as required. A voice then came from the tabernacle and said to her: "Have the Mass celebrated; that suffices."

And I too, I will take, to offer You in *infinite* thanksgiving, the Blood of this same sacrifice that redeemed and saved me. Receive it, Lord Jesus, as You received in the bosom of Your Father the sacrifice of Abel, and do not ever permit that I lose through my infidelity the fruit of Your passion and death.

XVIII

That this love of the Redeemer is wondrously manifest in all the goods with which His Heart has filled us

The mercy of Our Lord snatched me from sin and from hell. But this is only the negative side of what His infinite love deigned to do for me. On the positive side, the good that He merited for me is yet a thousand times more precious. If He delivered me from *all evil*, it was to give me *all good*. Yes, all good; for, with His heaven, with His beatitude and eternity, He gives Himself to me; and as He said to the holy Angela of Foligno, He is *"the All-Good."*

What a good, you say, is the possession of heaven, in other words, of perfect and eternal happiness, of perfect and eternal joy, of perfect and eternal love? Heaven is the bosom of God, in which the deified creature finds itself immersed with Jesus Christ, through Jesus Christ, and in Jesus Christ, in the ocean of divine light and eternal beatitude. Heaven is Love having become our life, our state, our atmosphere, our everything. No more fears, no more darkness, no more privations, no more failings, no more separations, no more tears, no more sufferings; but on the contrary the immeasurable, unchanging superabundance of every good, be it of the mind, the heart, or the senses. With Jesus, with Mary, with the blessed seraphim, cherubim, archangels, and holy angels, with all the saints, with all the elect, seeing God face to face, possessing God entirely, enjoying God, being filled with God's peace and joy; and this forever, without worry, without the possibility of losing a single tiny drop of this ocean of happiness. O my God, my God, what a prospect!

What happiness, what a good to be eternally the companion of the angels, living the life of the angels, being clothed in the glory of the angels, enjoying the felicity of the angels; in a word, of being *"as the angels"* (Mt 22:30; Mk 12:25; Lk 20:36)!

What a happiness and what a good to be forever in the rank of the sons of God, to be eternally the glorified members of God's only Son, His coheirs and His brethren (Rom 8:17)!

What a good and what happiness to be, with Jesus, kings of an eternal kingdom, and to possess the same kingdom that the Father of Jesus has given to His Son! And to sit at His table, with Mary, and with all the elect! What a glory to be clothed in the heavenly mantle of light, in the royal and glorious habit of the King of kings (Lk 22:29-30; Jn 17:22)!

In heaven, we will sit on one same throne with the Sovereign Monarch of earth and heaven (Rv 3:21). We will repose with our Savior in the bosom and adorable heart of His divine Father (Jn 17:24; 1:18). We will be the masters of all God's possessions (Mt 24:47). Finally, we will all be transformed into God (2 Cor 3:18), that is filled and penetrated with all of God's perfections, more intimately than the iron immersed into the furnace is clothed and penetrated with the qualities of fire. In Jesus Christ, we will become one with God, not through unity but through union; what God is by nature and essence, we will be through grace and participation.

O Lord, what a good, what a happiness is heaven! And yet everything I know of it is nothing in comparison with the reality. It is You Yourself Who have told me: *"Eye hath not seen, nor ear heard, neither hath it entered into the heart of man what things God hath prepared for them that love Him*" (1 Cor 2:9)!

Now, the unknown immensity of this heavenly and incomprehensible treasure, to what do I owe it? To the merciful and infinite love of the Heart of my Savior. In giving Himself to me, He has given me everything He has on earth: His Church, His Vicar, His truth, His sacraments, His Eucharist, His Body and Blood, His Mother, His Holy Cross, all His graces, all His spiritual riches; and in heaven He awaits me to be Himself my beatitude and immeasurable reward.

Thanks, therefore, infinite thanks to the Heart of my God, "for His unspeakable gift" (2 Cor 9:15)!

Yes, I have everything in Jesus Christ; and in His Sacred Heart, where I repose if am faithful to Him, is the abyss of all good, which snatches me from the abyss of all evil.

O good Jesus, forgive all those who do not love You. Alas, how great is their number! Is it not true, even in Christian countries, that many men treat this adorable Savior as if they had received nothing from Him? Is it not true that they treat Him almost as an enemy, forgetting Him, blaspheming Him, neglecting His service, mocking His priests, His Vicar, and His holy Church, laughing at confession, scoffing at His Eucharist, sometimes even going so far as to vulgarly insult His Most Holy Mother?

And yet what more could He have done to show His love for them?[1] "If it were possible," He one day told St. Bridget, "if it were possible that I suffer the torments of

---

[1] "What is there that I ought to do more to my vineyard, that I have not done to it?" (Is 5:4).

My Passion as many times as there are souls in hell, I would most willingly suffer them." And in return, most of those He has redeemed and enriched with His gifts crucify Him anew. Yes, they crucify Him, for whoever sins mortally is "*crucifying again to themselves the Son of God*" (Heb 6:6) and "*hath trodden underfoot the Son of God, and hath esteemed the blood of the testament unclean, by which he was sanctified*" (Heb 10:29).

O my God! If the least of all men happens to show us some affection, if he renders us the least service, we cannot help but love him; nay, if but an animal, if but a poor dog becomes attached to us and is a little useful to us, we love it. And our good God, Who is our Creator, our merciful Redeemer, our most faithful friend, our most good brother, our treasure, our glory, our sovereign good, our life, our heart, and Who is all heart and all love for us, would we not love Him?

XIX

That the Sacred Heart of Jesus loves us as His Father loves Him

On the same day as the institution of the Eucharist, still being in the Cenacle, Our Lord told His disciples something indeed amazing. It came from the depths of His Heart like a burning flame. "*I love you,*" He said, "*ego dilexi vos*" (Jn 15:9). Let us pause here. Let us ponder well this statement: "I love you."

Oh, how sweet it is! How sweet it is on the lips of the sovereign Lord of the universe, the Master of eternity!

Oh, how good and consoling it is! "I love you," our most good Jesus says.

If a great king deigned to enter one day into the cottage of the least of his subjects to tell him, "I love you; I have come here specifically to tell you this," what a joy for that poor man!

If an angel from heaven or a saint, or if even the Immaculate Virgin Mary, the Queen of Saints, deigned to suddenly appear to some poor sinner and tell him publicly, in the presence of everyone, "I love you, and my heart is yours," what transports and what raptures for that poor sinner!

Now, here is something infinitely greater. Here is the King of kings, the Holy of Holies, the sovereign Lord of heaven, having purposely come down from heaven to tell us here below, us, poor sinners: "*I love you, ego dilexi vos. Ego*, I Who am the Creator of all things, I Who govern the entire universe, I Who possess all the treasures of heaven and earth, I Who do everything that I will and Whose will no one can resist, I love you!"

O my good Savior, what a consolation! Would it not already be much to have told us, "I think about you sometimes, I cast My eyes on you once per year, I have some good plans for you"? But no, You want to assure us that You love us, and that Your divine Heart is full of tenderness for us; for us, I say, who are nothing; for us, earthworms, miserable ingrates who have crucified You and have merited hell so many times!

But in what manner does this adorable Heart of the Savior love us? Listen: "*Sicut dilexit me Pater*; *as the Father hath loved Me, I also have loved you* (Jn 15:9); I love you with the same Heart, with the same love with which I am loved by My Father."

And what is this love with which this divine Father loves His Son? It is a love having four great qualities which are consequently found in the love Jesus has for us.

First, it is an *infinite* love, meaning boundless, without limits and without measure; an incomprehensible and unspeakable love; a love as great as the very essence of God. Measure, if you can, the extent and greatness of the divine essence, and you will measure the greatness of the love of the Father for His Son Jesus; only then can you measure the greatness and extent of the love of Jesus for us.

Secondly, the love of the Father for His Son is an *eternal* love. Eternity is the duration of what is without variation, without change; it is what lasts forever, without beginning and without end. O Jesus, Eternal Word, this indeed is the love that You deserve, and that makes up for the failures in the love of all Your creatures, whether rebellious or simply weak, languid, and inconstant.

Now, it is this same eternal love with which Jesus is loved by His Father, with which we have the happiness of being loved by Jesus; for, one must not forget, in His Incarnation and while having assumed true humanity, He remains the second person of the Trinity, the eternal person of the only Son of God. He therefore loves us with a truly eternal love.

Eternity will not be too long to return love for love, an endless love for an eternal love. And in time, what are we doing? Are we loving Jesus Christ? Alas, are we not wasting this precious time, the seed of eternity, in loving the earth and the earth's trifles? What ingratitude!

In the third place, the love of the heavenly Father for His Son is a *universal* love, that is a love that fills all the hearts of heaven and earth. This love fills heaven, for the Father loves Jesus through the hearts of all the angels and all the blessed. It fills the earth, for it is again the Father Who loves Jesus Christ through the hearts of all the faithful. Indeed, what basically is this divine love of the Father for the Son, and of the Son for the Father, if not substantial and personal love, the Spirit of love, the Holy Ghost?

It is with this same love that my Savior deigns to love me. It is this same Spirit Who has been given to us all, and Who pours forth this same love into all our hearts.[1] Jesus loves me through the heart and in the heart of the Blessed Virgin, of St. Joseph, of each of His angels, and of each of His saints. What vastness! He loves me through the heart and in the heart of every member of His Church, beginning through the pope, through my bishop, through all the priests who love and care for my soul, and through all those who pray for me and do me good.

That is not all. As an effect of this admirable and universal law, He forbids all men, under the pain of sin and damnation, from harming my soul, my body, my reputation, or my property. Moreover, He commands all men to be truly brothers to me, loving me as themselves. Is it possible to extend love's solicitude any further?

And in this way, as St. Augustine says, heaven and earth and all they contain do not cease telling me that I should love my God.[2] He loves me everywhere; and I, an ingrate, offend Him everywhere! Oh, no longer allow it,

---

[1] "The charity of God is poured forth in our hearts, by the Holy Ghost who is given to us" (Rom 5:5).
[2] *The Confessions* 10.6.—Trans.

O most good Savior! See to it, rather, that I love and bless You everywhere.

Finally, the love of the Father for the Son is an *essential* and total love, meaning a love of His whole being. This divine Father loves His Son Jesus with all that He is, being all heart and all love for Him. The love that Jesus deigns to bear us is also an essential love, a total love; He loves us with all that He is and all that He has. All that is in Him, His divinity, His humanity, His soul, His body, His blood, all His thoughts, words, actions, privations, humiliations, and sufferings, His life, His death, His merits, and His glory; in a word, all that is in Him is employed to love us.

Above all, He employs His Sacred Heart to love us; and He has declared to numerous saints, especially to the renowned St. Bridget, whose revelations enjoy such great merit in the Church, that on the cross this adorable Heart had broken under the pressure of sorrow and love. *"My Heart"* Jesus told her, *"was immersed in an ocean of sufferings. I saw My Mother and those I loved overwhelmed with affliction; under the violence and strain of the sorrow, My Heart broke; and it was then that My soul separated from My body."*

Great God! And it was for me that these divine marvels were accomplished; that "decease"[1] of which Moses and Elias spoke with Jesus in glory on Tabor, it was I, a most unworthy sinner, who was its purpose! Jesus Christ loves me as His Father loves Him, with the same love with which He is loved by His Father, with an infinite, eternal, universal, and essential love!

---

[1] "Moses and Elias... spoke of his decease that he should accomplish in Jerusalem" (Lk 9:30-31).

When then will I open my eyes to no longer lose sight of the love My Savior bears me? Will I not then love with all my heart this good Jesus, Who deigns to love me so much, and Who, to yet more surely obtain my heart, promises me an eternity of beatitude if I consent to return Him love for love? And, as if that were not yet enough, He threatens me with hell's eternal fires if I refuse to love Him.

O Jesus, I therefore from now on want to love You as You love me: totally, without restriction, truly, and with *all* my heart. Have compassion on my weakness, which so often makes me falter in this nevertheless very sincere intention. I ask the Blessed Virgin to help me to be henceforth constantly and completely faithful to You.

XX

What the adorable Heart of Jesus suffered for us in His passion

All our Savior's passible and mortal life was a continuous exercise of charity, mercy, and suffering for each one of us. But it was especially at the time of His holy Passion that He showed us this love more.

That is when He elected to suffer dreadful torments, in His body and in His heart, to deliver us from the frightful tortures of hell and to acquire for us the immortal bliss of paradise. That is when we see His adorable body all covered with wounds and all bathed in blood; His sacred head, pierced with sharp thorns; His feet and His hands, transpierced by the nails. His divine flesh is all torn, all in bloody shreds; His body is stretched and dislocated on the Cross. All His senses are overwhelmed with horrors and pains. Finally, the cruelty of men, by dint of torments, tears His soul from His body, and rushing to Him, even after His death, one of these sinners thrusts his lance into His side and opens His heart.

But if, for our love, Jesus suffered so much in His body, if His body was torn and covered with wounds in this way, the pains of His soul, the invisible wounds of His Sacred Heart, were much more frightful still.

One could well count the wounds of His body; but those of His Heart, who would be able to count them? And what are these mysterious wounds?

They are firstly the wounds that all the world's sins inflicted upon Him. One day Our Lord showed St. Catherine of Genoa, in a sensible and symbolic form, the horror of the least venial sin. She asserted that although this vision lasted but a moment, she immediately fell into a kind of agony and would have died on the spot if God had not supernaturally sustained her. "If I were plunged into fire," she said, "and in order to get out of it I had to again see what was shown to me that day, I would prefer to stay in the fire." What then would she have experienced if she would have seen mortal sin?

Now, Jesus Christ, with a light that was infinitely greater since it was divine, saw in the depths of His agony, from the height of the Cross, *all* sins, mortal and venial, committed by all men and each one of them individually. These sins caused Him a horror that was equally divine, that is perfect and absolutely incomprehensible. Each of our sins was a deep wound for the Sacred Heart of Jesus. Count, if you can, all the sins that have been committed and will be committed on the earth throughout time from Adam and Eve until the Antichrist, and you will count the wounds of the Heart of Jesus.

Secondly, the wounds of this divine Heart are all those which pierced the bodies of His martyrs; they are all the sufferings and all the afflictions of the faithful, which Jesus suffers in His most good Heart, more than even they who endure them. Does not a mother suffer all the sufferings of her child, more so to speak than the child does? Now, the Heart of the Son of God being towards us of a truly infinite goodness and tenderness, consider the bitterness and depths of the sufferings of love which swooped upon Him, principally at the moment of His Passion!

Jesus therefore suffered all my sorrows, He bore all my pains, whatever they might be, of mind, heart, and body. They were so many very bloody wounds to His Sacred Heart. Oh, of how many mortal wounds have I been the cause, I alone, be it through my sins or through the thousand sorrows that have afflicted my life! Divine Jesus, how good You are! And how adorable is Your Heart!

Prostrate in spirit before Your Cross, from which salvation for me flows, I make two firm resolutions, which Your grace will help me to keep: the first, to guard myself more than ever against willingly falling again into sin, lest I be one of those of whom You spoke, O my Savior, through the mouth of Your Prophet: *They have added sorrows to My sorrows, wounds to My wounds.*[1] Oh, may I never again have this misfortune in the future!

---

[1] "They have added to the grief of my wounds" (Ps 68:27).

The second resolution is to unite myself with You in all my pains, whether interior or exterior, in order to sanctify them all and to draw consolation and life from where, for love of me, You drew desolation and death.

Most merciful Heart of Jesus, I give You thanks and recognize myself a thousand times unworthy of Your kindness.

XXI

The ineffable mercies of the Heart of Jesus in the sacrament of Penance

One might call the sacrament of Penance the marvel of the Heart of Jesus. There, indeed, more than in the other sacraments, He opens to all men this divine Heart which has loved them so much. There, more than anywhere else, the omnipotence of His mercy and goodness shines forth each day and throughout the earth, in miracles, healings, resurrections, and prodigies of all kinds.

Blessed Margaret Mary saw the Sacred Heart, with its fiery radiance, and with its cross and crown of thorns, as a throne all resplendent in glory. Is this throne not a beautiful image of the tribunal of Penance, where the glory of God shines no less in miracles of mercy than it shines on the altar in prodigies of love and holiness? What in fact is par excellence the glory of God on earth, if it is not the conversion of poor sinners and the resurrection and salvation of souls?

From the height of this throne of divine compassion and patience, incredible mercy, and inexhaustible forgiveness, the Heart of Jesus, living and beating in the hearts of His priests, burns with love for poor sinners and eagerly devours their sins in its divine flames. There it shines hope and pours forth the blood of redemption in great torrents.

The blood of Jesus, the blood of the Heart of Jesus, is like the soul of this great sacrament. It is a heavenly compound of holiness that purifies, tenderness that softens and consoles, compassion that touches and melts hearts, sacred ardors that warm, and finally, above all, loving charity. This is what confession is, this confession that is so frightening to those who do not have the happiness of believing in the love which the good God has for us.[1]

One day, upon returning from confession, St. Catherine of Siena wrote this profound statement: "I went to the blood of Christ, *ivi ad sanguinem Christi.*" To go to the blood of Jesus, is this not to go to His Heart, meaning to the source and hearth of His love? And there are men, Christians, who are scared of it! O divine blood, blood of love and infinite mercy! It is precisely because I am a sinner that I run to you. It is for me that you flow; it is for me that you wait, like the father of the prodigal child waited for his poor son. Yes, I shall go to you, O purifying and sanctifying blood! I shall go to you with a most contrite and most humbled heart certainly, but also with a heart full of confidence. What a joy to have this treasure of confession! And how truly it is the Spouse of Jesus Christ, this merciful Catholic Church, which possesses the throne of mercy of the Heart of Jesus!

---

[1] "And we have known and have believed the charity which God hath to us" (1 Jn 4:16).

The sacrament of Penance, one can say, is the triumph of the Sacred Heart of Jesus. He appears even much more abundantly merciful here than in the sacrament of Baptism: in Baptism (at least for infants), the grace of forgiveness only effaces a stain for which the sinner is not personally responsible; in Penance, this same grace widens, widens yet again, and knows no other limits than those imposed on it by the bad will of those sad madmen we call impenitent sinners. It is of faith that in the sacrament of confession everything, without exception, everything, absolutely everything, can be forgiven by the priest; and the Church wants the priest to forgive everything, from the moment the sinner gives true signs of repentance. O mercy of the Savior! The same is true for relapses, provided they are due only to frailty and weakness. Jesus calls the weak like the strong to forgiveness, the poor like the rich, all those who have good will. After the altar, which is the throne of holy love, the priest of Jesus is nowhere greater and more admirable than in the confessional, the throne of holy mercy.

The flames with which the Sacred Heart burns there do not only devour our sins, but they totally destroy and annihilate them; they additionally devour and annihilate for us the eternal flames of hell that were due to these sins; and the Church even teaches that if our contrition is perfect, the flames of the merciful Heart of Jesus also devour and destroy there the terrible flames of purgatory.

Through its loving flames, the Heart of Jesus simultaneously inflames, expands, and liquefies both the heart of the confessor, whom these flames fill with charity and gentleness, and the heart of the penitent, whom they fill with contrition, purify even to its tiniest recesses, and inundate with happiness and joy.

And all of this is the fruit of the cross and of the crown of thorns; it is the fruit of the Passion of Jesus Christ, whose infinite merits the sacrament of Penance applies to us.

Make me then, O my most good Savior, to love this wondrous sacrament as I ought, and to have recourse to it often, with a great desire to profit much from the holy outpourings of Your blood there. Make me to always confess well, to be truly sincere in the admission of my sins and truly loyal to my conscience, to tread upon pride and human considerations, and to always receive absolution with the strong dispositions Your Sacred Heart communicates to all the hearts of its faithful and wants to see radiate in them.

XXII

The Sacred Heart and the Blessed Sacrament

The Sacred Heart of Jesus is amidst us on earth, at the same time that it is in heaven. Inseparable from the most holy and most adorable humanity of Jesus Christ, whose center and life it is, this divine Heart, so loving and so loved, resides in each of our churches, beneath the veil of the Eucharist. And this is of faith.

We too often forget the reality of this living presence of Our Lord on earth. All of us believe it in theory (otherwise we would be heretics), but we do not all believe it in practice; and this is perhaps the principal cause of that lukewarmness, and of those thousand and one failings we are the first to lament. We do not have, at least not in the measure needed, *the spirit of faith* in the very real and very living presence of Our Lord Jesus Christ in the Eucharist.

The same is true with respect to His Sacred Heart. We easily look at it as a kind of heavenly abstraction, very beautiful to contemplate from afar, but inaccessible. If we had a livelier faith, we would see it present on the altar, in the middle of Jesus's sacred chest. What graces this living faith would draw to our souls!

From within the tabernacle, Jesus Christ waits for us and calls us. Like to Blessed Margaret Mary, He shows to us and at the same time opens to us His Heart ablaze with love: "Behold," He tells us, "behold this Heart which has loved men so much; and in return for My love, I receive from them only ingratitude and insults!" The altar is in fact the throne of divine love, like the tribunal of Penance is the throne of divine mercy. From the height of the latter, the Heart of Jesus opens to forgive and purify; from the height of the former, it gives itself substantially and it opens to love, strengthen, and sanctify.

At the altar, the priest of Jesus holds in his consecrated hands the Body and the Heart of the Son of God; and in the holy chalice, he contemplates and drinks the very Blood that, from the Sacred Heart, vivified the flesh of the Incarnate Word. And as the Eucharist is above all the mystery of love, one can say that the Catholic priest is truly the consecrator, depositary, and dispenser of the Sacred Heart of Jesus.

Each day in communion he receives in himself this divine Heart, this adorable Blood. He receives it, and we ourselves when we go to communion receive it, with all its flames, with all its blazing. Oh, what a hearth of love is communion, where one eats and drinks Eternal Love,

Jesus Christ, the glorified flesh, Heart, and Blood of Jesus Christ!

What the love of our Savior does in the mystery of the Eucharist is such a cumulation of marvels, that instead of speaking of it, one would be tempted out of respect to stay silent and adore. Everything one can say of it is nothing.

St. Bernard calls this great sacrament the love of loves, "*amor amorum.*" It is love indeed, and love alone, that impels Our Lord to enclose Himself under this humble appearance, stripped of all luster, and to remain this way on this earth of miseries, sludge, and impurities, exposed to a thousand and a thousand insults, and this for the past nineteen centuries and until the Antichrist, until the second coming.

It is love which makes Jesus remain in our midst, to cover us in the eyes of His heavenly Father, like the hen covers her chicks with her wings and protects them. There, on the altar, His divine Heart supplying for the infirmity of His Church militant, raises unceasingly towards Heaven adoration, praise, thanksgiving, supplications, and prayers absolutely worthy of the divine majesty. "*Always living to make intercession for us*" (Heb 7:25), He loves for us, He obtains for us. He blesses us with unceasing benedictions, according to these beautiful words of St. Peter: "*God hath sent you His Son to bless you*" (Acts 3:26).

It is love which has made Him encapsulate in the Blessed Sacrament all His mysteries of mercy and tenderness;[1] for He is there, beneath the Eucharistic veil,

---

[1] "He hath made a remembrance of his wonderful works, being a merciful and gracious Lord; he hath given food to them that fear him" (Ps 110:4-5).

the eternal Creator and Lord of angels and men, of heaven and earth, the Sanctifier of all the elect, the Holy of Holies, the Head and Supreme Pontiff of the Church, the King of patriarchs and prophets, the Savior, and the Redeemer. He is there with the grace of the mystery of His Incarnation, with His long sacrifice of thirty-three and a half years, with all His words and all His miracles. He is there with all that He worked in the holy soul of His Mother, and in His Church and in all His elect. Finally, He is there with the entire world of grace and the entire world of glory, of which He is the principle, the center, and the life. What an ocean of love is the Eucharist!

And all this Mystery of mysteries, this love of loves, it is really just Your Sacred Heart, O my most sweet Jesus! Ingrates that we are, how will we respond to this prodigious goodness? We forget Him in the silence of His tabernacles, and most of those hearts for which He did all of this are colder, harder, and more unfeeling to Him than the marble of the altars, than the gold and the silver of the ciboria!

XXIII

How, in Holy Communion, the Heart of Jesus purifies, illuminates, and deifies us in His holy love

Imagine, if possible, all the charity and all the tenderness that have been, are, will be, and even could be in all the hearts that God's almighty hand could form; imagine them gathered and as though condensed into one heart vast enough to contain them. Now tell me, would that one heart not form a hearth of truly incomprehensible love? Well (and this is part of the faith), it would be nothing, so to speak, in comparison to the *infinite* love with which the eternal Son of God burns for us, for each one of us, in His Sacred Heart, and consequently in the Holy Sacrament of the altar.

Now, when we go to communion, we have the happiness of receiving in our body and in our soul this divine Jesus with the infinite treasure of His Heart and of His love. He enters us all ablaze, and what does He want, if not to set our very selves ablaze with the sacred fire with which He burns? *"I am come to cast fire on the earth. And what will I, but that it be kindled?"* (Lk 12:49).

To respond more easily to this desire of the Heart of Jesus, it must be known that the "fire" of which He speaks is a purifying fire, an illuminating fire, a sanctifying fire, a transforming fire, and finally, a deifying fire. It is the fire of His holy love.

It is a *purifying* fire. When we have the happiness to communicate piously, the sacred flames of the Heart of Jesus purify our soul of its least stains. Like gold cast into the furnace and melted in the blazing crucible, our soul melts with love in the Heart of Jesus, and the thousand imperceptible specks that debase its purity are consumed by the fire of divine love. Holy Communion was in fact instituted, the Council of Trent tells us, "to preserve us from mortal sins *and to deliver us from our daily faults.*" Those small venial faults, which elude human frailty, far from turning us away from frequent communion, ought rather to propel us there, like illness propels us towards the physician and the remedy. Communion is the direct remedy the heavenly Physician offers us to purify us and to rid us of our venial sins; and in Holy Communion, it is the fire of love that works this salutary purification.

Secondly, the fire of the Eucharistic Heart of Jesus is an *illuminating* fire. In His sacrament, Jesus is like the sun which brightens while it warms. Communion is an illuminating hearth of love which strengthens and augments the splendors of faith, which dispels the delusions and darkness by which hell unceasingly seeks to bedim our souls, and which makes us enter more and more into the admirable light of Jesus Christ,[1] into the splendid realities of the faith. It is especially in communion that we must confidently say to our Jesus: "*Lord, increase our faith; Domine, adauge nobis fidem*" (Lk 17:5). And He will lovingly open to us the treasures of heavenly light of which His divine Heart is the sun and the hearth.

Thirdly, the fire of Jesus's love is a *sanctifying* fire. It is not without reason that the reception of the sacrament of the Eucharist is called in the Church "*Holy* Communion" and "*Most Holy* Communion." It sanctifies us, that is, it detaches us from the earth by uniting us more and more to the King of heaven. It makes us live, it makes increase in us Jesus Christ, the Holy of Holies; and it nourishes all the virtues that constitute Christian holiness. The love of Jesus in the Eucharist is the true food of the imperfect who desire to become perfect, of penitent sinners determined to be faithful and most faithful in the future, and of the weak who want to become strong. O most holy Body! O most holy Heart of my God! Make me

---

[1] "Who hath called you out of darkness into his marvelous light" (1 Pt 2:9).

draw from my communions all the fruits of holiness which Your love has placed there.

Fourthly, the fire of the Heart of Jesus in Holy Communion is a *transforming* fire. Just as physical fire transforms gold, silver, and the hardest metals, turns solids into liquids, and makes the coarse and abrupt very fine, very pure, and very splendid, so does the fire of the holy love of Jesus Christ have our communions imperceptibly work a wondrous transformation in us. From worldly, they make us Christian and spiritual; from being negligent, lukewarm, and dissipated prior to frequenting the sacrament of love, they transform us little by little into interior, recollected, fervent, and zealous men. They change our tastes and the direction of our life; they make us meek and humble of heart, chaste, and devoted to our brethren; in short, they end up transforming us into other Jesus Christs; and by eating the Goodness, the Purity, and the Holiness that are nothing other than Jesus Christ Himself, they make us become supernaturally good, pure, and holy.

Finally, the fire of the Sacred Heart that inflames our souls when we receive Jesus Christ in communion is a *deifying* fire. Yes, the good God's grace and love go this far. We are called to participate in His divine nature, as He Himself says: "*divinae consortes naturae*" (2 Pt 1:4). And although grace already begins this deification at Baptism, it must nevertheless be recognized that, without Holy Communion, it could not develop nor even continue, just like the life we receive at birth could neither develop nor continue without the food that unceasingly feeds it.

"*You are gods and all of you the sons of the Most High,*" the Lord tells us (Ps 81:6). Is it surprising that gods, sons of God, receive as food the Body and Blood of the only Son of God, really and truly present under the appearance of bread in the Eucharist?

And all these marvels have but a single cause, which is Your adorable love, O my Savior! They flow from a single source, which is Your Sacred Heart, present and burning in the middle of Your heavenly humanity and contained with it in the great sacrament of the altar.

Oh, deign then to increase in me—and not only in me, but also in all your priests, in all your faithful, men, women, children, rich, poor, in all without exception—love, and what one could call the *meaning* of Holy Communion! Make us all to understand that to communicate is to love You; and that to communicate often and piously is to love You perfectly.

Glory and love to the Heart of Jesus in the most holy sacrament of the altar!

XXIV

That the Holy Ghost intimately unites our hearts to the Sacred Heart of Jesus

In the mystery of grace, Our Lord Jesus Christ, King of Heaven, deigns to unite Himself to us interiorly and spiritually, to communicate to us His divine life, His virtues, and His holiness. Grace is a mystery entirely of love; and it is a mystery of union, love tending always towards union.

Jesus, Who loves us, therefore unites us to Himself, not in a material, coarse, and imperfect union like the unions of the earth, but in an entirely heavenly union, a union entirely spiritual and divine; and this union, it is through the Holy Ghost and in the Holy Ghost that He works this. On behalf of His divine Father, He gives us through pure grace, through pure goodness, this adorable Spirit Who is Love and *Union* personified. It is quite simple that union unites, and therefore the first thing the Holy Ghost does in us when He is given to us in Baptism is to unite us to Jesus and through Jesus to God the Father. This union of grace is a union entirely of love, since it is born from the love of God and of Jesus; since it is worked through love itself, which is the Holy Ghost; and since it supremely aims to make us love with all our heart, strength, and soul Him Who deigns to love us so much.

This is a union that is spiritual, interior, sanctifying, supernatural, heavenly, and deifying; it is the life of our souls; it is the seed of heaven and the principle of eternal life.

Our heart is thereby united, through the Holy Ghost, through the Spirit of love, to the Sacred Heart of Jesus, Who wants to see us become completely like Himself, meaning all heavenly and all divine. Oh, what a beautiful mystery! My heart sees itself united to the Heart of its God; beginning in this world, it sees itself drawn, rooted, and fixed in heaven in the Sacred Heart of Jesus, Who will lovingly communicate to it the life of grace as a pledge of the glory He is preparing for it in Paradise! What perpetual adoration do I not owe to this divine Heart which lives and beats in my heart! And with what love must I recognize this treasure of love!

My heart is united to the Heart of Jesus, like the branch is united to the vine. Thanks to this union, the vine's sap passes into the branch, vivifies it, and communicates to it its properties. Separated from the vine, the branch is dead; it can no longer produce anything. United to the vine, it flowers, is covered with dense foliage, and produces beautiful, delicious bunches of grapes which the sun goldens and ripens. The heavenly Heart of Jesus is the vine, and my poor heart is the branch. The sap of the Heart of Jesus is the Holy Ghost, it is the Spirit of grace and love. From the Heart of Jesus, this divine Spirit passes and flows into my heart, and comes to spread into my understanding, my will, and all the powers of my soul the same dispositions and same sentiments that fill the Heart of my divine Master. He brings me His light, His strength, His goodness, His humility, His meekness, His patience, His purity, His adorable charity, His detachment, His love of sufferings, and His perfect holiness.

He makes my heart fruitful; He makes it produce the thousand leaves and sweet-smelling flowers of good thoughts, pious affections, and holy desires; He makes it produce abundant fruits, meaning all kinds of good works and precious sacrifices ripened and goldened by the sun of the Church, the Holy Sacrament of the altar. The mystery of grace is in fact inseparable from the mystery of the Eucharist; life is inseparable from the Bread of life; love calls for the Bread of love. Communion ripens and perfects the fruits of grace.

It is therefore in the depths of my heart that I must seek, in order to unite myself to it in love, Your adorable Heart, O my Savior Jesus Christ! It is there that I find the kingdom of God, Your kingdom, and that I find You Yourself Who reign within me in Your Spirit. *"The kingdom of God is within you"* (Lk 17:21). Oh, what a treasure! It is the treasure in the Gospel parable. To acquire it and to keep it, I will sell all that I possess, and I will buy the field that contains it. This field, it is Your grace; it is Your sweet and holy love.

O Heart of Jesus! Adorable and adored Heart, I wish to dwell in You all the days of my life, and unto eternal life, where Your mercy will admit me, all unworthy though I be.

Blessed be the Jesus of my heart! Blessed be the Heart of my Jesus!

XXV

An admirable example of this union of the faithful soul with the Sacred Heart of Jesus

In that same century when Providence raised up first Fr. Eudes and then Blessed Margaret Mary for the glorification of the Sacred Heart of Jesus, the mysteries of this adorable Heart were manifested to another very holy religious, a Carmelite, Sister Margaret of the Blessed Sacrament. This Margaret of Carmel was a precious flower, no less precious than the one in the flowerbed of the Visitation. Her sweet smell spread far; and St. Vincent de Paul, Fr. de Condren, and Fr. Olier held her in singular veneration.

Sister Margaret of the Blessed Sacrament received from Our Lord a grace similar to that of St. Gertrude, Fr. Eudes, and Blessed Margaret Mary. She united the Blessed Sacrament and the Sacred Heart in an equal love, and this love completely absorbed her.

Among the numerous supernatural favors with which Sister Margaret's life was filled, her biographer recounts that Jesus, one day uniting Himself to her yet more closely than in the past, opened to her His divine Heart and hid her in this Holy of Holies.

"He showed her His Heart as a vast and immense furnace of love in which He enclosed her day and night for a duration of more than three weeks. There, she drew so many graces from their very source, and she arrived at such a sanctity, that her progress seemed greater in a single day than it had previously been during entire years.

"At times this divine Heart, burning her entirely like a most intense fire, consumed in her her imperfections; at times she was plunged there as in an abyss of charity which inflamed her in such a way that her very body felt its heat; at times the love of Jesus swept her up with such forcefulness that she was seen lifted from the ground, beautiful and ablaze like a seraphim; at times she was immersed there as in a fountain of holiness; at times she found herself there as though dyed in innocence itself; and sometimes, finally, she was there all perfumed in purity.

"She noticed in the Heart of Jesus a double movement of expansion and contraction; and Jesus made her to understand that His Sacred Heart contracted so as to fill itself with the divine Spirit, to love His heavenly Father, to offer Himself to Him in sacrifice, to annihilate Himself before His divine majesty, to enter into His divine life, to unite Himself to all His adorable perfections, and to render Him all His obligations. It expanded, on the other hand, in order to pour forth His Spirit into all His members, and to communicate to His Church, which is His Body, the warmth of life.

"In this adorable Heart, she perceived an ocean without bottom and without borders, an ocean of love for God His Father, a possession and enjoyment of His divine goodness, a repose in His infinite beatitude, a calm and peace surpassing all understanding, an incomprehensible treasury of all the virtues, and they shined there in such great and ineffable beauty, loftiness, scope, and splendor that they could fill an infinity of worlds.

"She also saw how this divine Heart, amidst so many riches and beatitude, had been drowned in deep abysses of most bitter sufferings; that, beneath the weight of the sins of men, it had been as though crushed and reduced to agony; and that it would have succumbed if it had not been sustained by the omnipotence of the uncreated Word.

"But notwithstanding, she experienced in this most benign Heart such an admirable transport of love for those who had done Him so much harm that it cannot be expressed; it was the strength and generosity of this love that had caused the sweating of blood in the garden of Gethsemane.

"She saw this adorable Heart as the sacred palace where all the Savior's sentiments were born and nourished, all His affections, desires, joys, and sadness. However, among all these treasures of virtue and holiness, it was principally in love, purity of heart, and innocence that Sister Margaret was made a participant.

"The hold that Jesus more and more had on her each day consumed her so much that she no longer took almost any food. She found in the Heart of her Jesus a supernatural supplement that sustained her and restored her strength, more effective than the fruit in the earthly paradise could have done. It seemed to her at times that there flowed from this divine Heart into all her members a sacred and vivifying liquid, sometimes like a most gentle oil, sometimes like a most pure milk, sometimes like a balm emitting a heavenly perfume, and sometimes, finally, like a delightful manna that fortified not only her body, but also produced in her soul marvelous effects.

"This fully hidden life within the Sacred Heart was not, we believe, a sensible transport of the body, but only of the soul; and this entry Jesus gave her into His Heart was a loving invention of mercy, in order to more closely associate her with His divine innocence."

Such was the supernatural and miraculous union of Venerable Sister Margaret of the Blessed Sacrament with the Sacred Heart of the Son of God. Although Jesus does not grant equally extraordinary graces to all His faithful, it is nevertheless certain that all those who sincerely love Him with all their heart are truly united to His Sacred Heart in the mystery of grace. The same Spirit Who works the miraculous unions of which the lives of the saints offer us so many examples, works in us, when we are faithful, a most real, most intimate, most profound, and all heavenly union with Our Lord Jesus Christ, and most especially with His adorable Heart.

Let us humbly content ourselves to be united to Jesus through this common path in the Church, which is the path of faith; and when we want to love or adore the good God, to conceive a true sorrow for our sins, to render to our heavenly Father the duties of religion He expects from our fidelity, let us turn interiorly towards the divine Heart of Jesus, unite ourselves to it through prayer and love, enter into it, and remain in and be but one with it, praying and adoring with this Heart, loving all that it loves, and detesting and rejecting all that it reproves.

Therefore, glory, love, and thanksgiving to this most kind and most merciful Heart of our Savior, for all the graces and blessings He has poured forth and will pour forth until the end of time on earth and in heaven, in all the hearts that love Him and that will love Him eternally!

XXVI

That Jesus gives us His Heart to be our heart

Our adorable Mediator Jesus Christ, wanting to render His Father in all His mystical members and in each one of them individually the homages of a perfect religion truly worthy of Him, unites Himself interiorly with all Christians and gives them His Heart. He gives us this great and ineffable Heart so that, through Him and with Him, we might render to God all our duties and fulfill all our obligations towards His divine majesty.

We are obliged to five great duties with respect to the good God: first, to adore Him in His infinite greatness; second, to give Him thanks for the incredible goods we have received and continuously receive from His goodness; third, to satisfy His most holy justice for our innumerable sins and negligences; fourth, to love Him in return for His incomprehensible love; and fifth, finally, to pray with humility and trust to obtain from His supreme liberality everything that is necessary for us, whether for soul or body.

Now, how can we discharge all these duties in a manner worthy of God? This is impossible for us: only the infinite is worthy of the infinite; only the divine is worthy of the divine. If we had at our disposal all the minds, hearts, and strength of all angels and men, and if we used them to adore, thank, and love the Lord, it would still be a little thing in relation to His infinite holiness and goodness.

But here is a means, an infinitely infinite means for completely fulfilling all these duties: it is the very Heart of Jesus which is given us so that we can use it as our own heart, to adore God as much as He is adorable, to love Him as much as He deserves to be loved, and to render Him all the duties of most perfect religion in a manner absolutely worthy of His supreme majesty.

Eternal thanks be Yours, O my dear Savior Jesus, for this infinitely precious gift of Your Heart. May the angels and the Queen of Angels help me to bless You for this! Oh, how rich we are! And what treasures we possess!

The Heart of Jesus, which has become *our* heart, has us participate in the eternal love with which the Father loves the Son, and with which the Son loves the Father. The Father loves us as He loves Jesus;[1] and in turn, Jesus loves us with the same love that unites Him to His divine Father.[2] And in this way, in You, in Your Heart, O Jesus, we are, we also, "*consummated in one,*"[3] as You and Your Father are consummated in one through love and in love, through the Holy Ghost and in the Holy Ghost. Oh, what depths of divine tenderness!

Moreover, I find in the Heart of my God the means to most perfectly love all I must love outside of God, but

---

[1] "Thou hast loved them, as thou hast also loved me" (Jn 17:23).
[2] "As the Father hath loved me, I also have loved you" (Jn 15:9).
[3] "*Consummati in unum*" (Jn 17:23).

according to God: first, and above all, the Most Blessed Virgin, whom I can only love worthily with the help of the Heart of her divine Son; then, all my brethren in heaven and all my brethren on earth. It is said of Jesus Christ's first faithful that they had "but one heart and one soul" (Acts 4:32); that single heart was the Heart of Jesus having become their heart; it was the meeting of their most holy, most pure, most penitent, most charitable, most meek, and most humble hearts in the Sacred Heart of Jesus, which was in this way their most singular hearth of love and their heavenly meeting place. It was to them the center of a sphere where all the radii originating from the surface come to meet, in order to form but a single point in this center.

And I also, a poor little radius in the great sphere of the Church, I rush towards you, I give myself to You, I want always to dwell in you, O adorable and adored Heart of my God! There I find the means to superabundantly love what I must love, in heaven and on earth, in eternity as in time. There I am certain to love piously, to love perfectly, and also to be loved myself as I ought to be loved, no more and no less.

But what will I do in practice to remain in this way in the Heart of Jesus? How, in what concerns me, will my poor heart and that divine Heart be but one heart? I will apply myself to two things: First, in the details of my life, my duties, and my daily actions, I will endeavor to deny myself, "*abneget semetipsum*"; to renounce not only the guilty inclinations, but the base and natural ones of my own heart, which due to original sin is instinctively diverted from the true and the good, and turned towards evil. Then, I will take great care to live in habitual and interior union with Jesus, in order to let His Sacred Heart live, desire, love, suffer, and expand in my heart, with my heart, and, so to speak, in the place of my heart.

O Heart of my Savior, Who are all love, be from now on, until my last breath, the true heart of my heart, the soul of my soul, the mind of my mind, and the life of my life; be the single driving force of all my faculties, thoughts, words, and actions.

The venerable servant of God, Marie-Eustelle [Harpain], this humble and renowned little laborer from Saintes known to all of France, walked in this light and lived this life. The Heart of Jesus was truly her heart; the will of Jesus Christ was her will. "How shall I express," she wrote at the end of the memoir of her interior life which obedience had imposed upon her, "how shall I express the love and attraction Jesus gave me for this total loss of my will in His own? It is my paradise, it is my delight; it sweetens everything, makes me bear everything, acquiesce to everything, and rejoice at and in everything. When the sweet Jesus wants something of me, He shows me His merciful Heart, and with a sweet majesty He affectionately tells me, '*Such is My good pleasure.*'

"When He required some sacrifice of me," Marie-Eustelle further stated, "He presented Himself to my soul in His sacred humanity, and He showed me His Heart whilst saying to me, '*It is from here that this or that desire comes; it is from here that I invite you to this or that sacrifice.*' Therefore, I was overflowing with joy when I had something to suffer; and, for the love of this good divine pleasure, I would have accepted the cruelest and most ignominious death, after an entire life of sufferings.

"O my Jesus, my heavenly and peaceful friend!... O Jesus, how good You are! You give me the foretaste of heavenly felicity even in this life, so inexpressible are the sweetnesses with which You fill my soul!

"O Jesus, the love of my heart, I desire no book other than Your divine Heart!"

XXVII

That the adorable Heart of Jesus is our refuge and our oracle

Our most good Savior did not only give us His Heart to be the object of our homage, adoration, and love; He also gave it to us to be our refuge and our oracle.

The Heart of Jesus is our *refuge*. We have great need of a refuge in this miserable world. Everything here is a tempest, a storm, a peril, and a war to death. The world, meaning the totality of creatures who in one way or another participate in Satan's great revolt against Jesus Christ and His Church, the world resembles a raging sea, amidst which we must attain the shore of blessed eternity. The little barque of our soul is at all times subject to shipwreck. Alas, how many of these barques, after having resisted the impact of the waves, end up sinking and perishing!

However, amidst this tempest, the divine mercy has arranged for us a refuge, a port of salvation: it is the Sacred Heart of Jesus. This most holy and most peaceful Heart shelters us from the waves and the tempests. We find here a heavenly calm which the lightning and thunder cannot trouble. We taste here the chaste delights that have no bitterness; a joy that no sadness can alter; a light without obscurity, a most smooth sweetness, a serenity without clouds. It is this Heart that is the first principle of all good, the divine sanctuary of the Holy Ghost, the principal source of all joys, and of all the beatitude of Paradise.

Let us then take refuge in this port of salvation and grace, towards which the Star of the Sea, that is, the most holy and immaculate Virgin Mary, lovingly guides us. Let us have recourse to the Heart of Jesus in all our difficulties and in all our affairs. Let us go find there *"the peace of God which surpasseth all understanding"* (Phil 4:7), *"the peace of [Jesus] Christ [which] rejoice[s] your hearts"* (Col 3:15). Let us seek there our consolation in sadness, strength in our trials, fidelity and perseverance in our temptations. Let us seek there the sanctification of our joys. Let us take cover there from the wickedness of men, from the assaults of our passions, and from the snares of the demon. Let us hide and take shelter in this sacred refuge where divine justice itself loses its rights and is transformed into mercy.

The Heart of Jesus is our *oracle*. In the Tabernacle of Moses, there was over the ark of the covenant, between the two large golden cherubim which covered it with their wings, a large strip of wonderfully polished and shining pure gold called the Oracle or the Propitiatory. It was here that reposed "the glory of the Lord," that is to say the Word, the Word of God; and it was from here that the Lord spoke to Moses, making known to him His will, and enlightening, supporting, and consoling him in his daily difficulties.

This *oracle* of the ancient Temple was the prophetic symbol of Jesus Christ, and in particular of His most holy and most divine Heart. For us Christians, our "oracle" is no longer cold and unfeeling gold, but rather the living humanity, the living and all heavenly Heart of the Son of God, of this same Word Who spoke in times past in the Holy of Holies of the Tabernacle. In the law of grace, everything is living, everything is "spirit and life" (Jn 6:64).

O Jesus, true Holy of Holies, what an "oracle" You present to Your faithful! Your Heart, Your Sacred Heart, this is our Oracle, our Propitiatory. The one in ancient Israel was only in a single place; ours is everywhere You are; it is in each one of our churches, in each consecrated Host; it covers the world. And even more than that: each one of us, when he is faithful to You, can reach it in his own heart, with the two powerful hands of faith and love; he can reach it in heaven, through prayer; he is able to never separate from it, through union and the life of grace, through habitual recollection, and through purity of heart and adoration.

The Oracle of Israel only lasted for a time; ours will last eternally. Over the Oracle of the Temple, the Divine Word spoke to Moses through the ministry of angels (Gal 3:19). From the very depths of Your Heart, it is You, You in person, Lord Jesus, Who deign to speak to us face to face and heart to heart, like a friend to a friend.

It is from here, through the secret inspirations of His grace, that our most good God enlightens and directs our consciences, makes known to us His will, allays our fears, and soothes our sadness, when we have recourse to Him with humility and trust.

On every occasion, let us then have recourse to the adorable Heart of Jesus; let us implore it and consult it. Let us celebrate if we are priests, or let us have celebrated if we are not, the Holy Mass in its honor; let us make our communions with this same intention, and we shall unfailingly experience the effects of its goodness.

Let us always adore it, similar to those two golden cherubim, both bowing over the Oracle of the Temple, showing through this holy attitude what was to one day be the blessed adorers of the divine Heart of Jesus.

XXVIII

How the Sacred Heart is the model our hearts must follow

It is a truth beyond doubt that the King of Heaven, Jesus Christ, loves us so mercifully that each of us can say with full assurance: "The Heart of my Jesus is mine; I possess the Heart of my Savior."

Yes, this living treasure of love is mine. It is mine because His eternal Father has given it to me; it is mine because the Blessed Virgin, His Mother, has given it to me; it is mine because the Holy Ghost has given it to me and intimately united me to it in the ineffable mystery of grace; finally, it is mine because this good Savior Himself has given it to me a thousand and a thousand times.

He has given it to me not only to be my refuge and my oracle, but also to be the model and rule of my life and my actions. It is this most holy model that I want to look at and study continuously, in order to faithfully imitate it.

Now, what is it I find in the adorable Heart of Jesus Christ? It is of extreme importance that I know this very clearly, so that I might love what He loves and detest what He detests. Here is what the Gospel teaches me of this, as well as the Church and the saints.

The Heart of Jesus has never hated or rejected anything except evil, that is to say sin in all its forms. Did He have the least hatred for His persecutors and executioners? Not at all; on the contrary, He excused them before His Father at the very moment of their terrible deicide. "*Father, forgive them, for they know not what they do*" (Lk 23:34). This is the rule I want to follow from now on, O my good Master! Like You and with You, I want to hate nothing except sin; for love of You, I will love those who hate me, I will forgive them with all my heart, and strive to always return them good for evil.

The Heart of Jesus detested, with all the energy of His divine holiness, the Pharisees, hypocrites, enemies of truth, and seducers of souls. With Him and like Him, I will detest the impious and the blasphemers, the enemies of the faith, of the Church, and of the Holy See; I will love their souls and pray for their conversion; however, insofar as they remain vassals of evil, I will "hate them with a perfect hatred" (Ps 138:22). I will detest them and fight them, as Jesus Christ fights them and detests them. Indeed, in the Heart of Jesus, is not the holy horror of evil and of those who do evil as equally lively as the holy love of good and of those who do good? To behave otherwise would not be charity, it would be weakness; it would be lax complacency.

The Heart of my God being my model, I must, according to the precept of St. Paul, have in my heart all the sentiments that filled His own.[1] Otherwise, I will not have His Spirit, and I will not be His.[2]

What are these sentiments?

They are firstly the sentiments of ineffable love Jesus has for His Father and for the most holy will of His Father. He has such love for His divine will that, during the entire course of His life, He never did His own will, completely perfect as it was, but uniquely and lovingly the will of His heavenly Father. He says to us, "*I always do the things that please Him*" (Jn 8:29); "*My meat is to do the will of Him that sent Me*" (Jn 4:34).

It is secondly the sentiment of horror and appalment we just spoke of, relating to sin, and which made Him prefer all kinds of humiliations and sufferings rather than letting it reign in the world. Fought to the extreme by Jesus Christ and His faithful, sin, even when it triumphs momentarily, is defeated in advance; and the day is coming when it will be absolutely extirpated from the earth. After the example of Our Lord and with the help of His grace, I will suffer everything from now on rather than voluntarily commit a single sin, even a venial one.

Thirdly, they are the sentiments of love He has for the cross and for sufferings. His Sacred Heart was, so to speak, even more crucified than His flesh: the Heart of Jesus Crucified is the deepest of the depths of the cross. Jesus thus loves suffering so much that the Holy Ghost, speaking of the day of His Passion, calls it the day of the joy of the Heart of Jesus, "*in die laetitiae cordis ejus*" (Sg

---

[1] "For let this mind be in you, which was also in Christ Jesus" (Phil 2:5).
[2] "Now if any man have not the Spirit of Christ, he is none of his" (Rom 8:9).

3:11). He does not love sufferings or humiliations in themselves, for they are an evil; He loves them, He calls for them, and He bears them joyfully, on account of the divine effects they produce. It is thus for Your love and for Your salvation that I want to love crosses, O Jesus!

There are then the sentiments of love He has for His beloved Mother. We have already stated that He loves her, her alone, more than He loves all His angels and saints combined.

There are also the sentiments of charity, kindness, and compassion He has for us, and in a very special way for the little and the humble, for children, the unfortunate, the poor, and the afflicted.

Finally, what faith reveals to me in the adorable Heart of Jesus is a profound sentiment of contempt and hatred for the corruption, vanities, and follies of the world. He so much detests the world, that is to say the creatures who are united with Satan against God, that He formally curses it. *"Woe to the world because of scandals!"* (Mt 18:7). He states that the world is to Him as one excommunicated! *"I pray not for the world"* (Jn 17:9). He tells His disciples that "they are not of the world" any more than He Himself is "of the world" (Jn 17:16). And this is very simple. What indeed is the world, if not a satanic ensemble of pride and vanity, greed and curiosity, impurity and sensuality?[1]

These are the sentiments that filled the Heart of Jesus; these are the sentiments with which He desires, and I too desire, to see my heart filled. My God, my God, grant me

---

[1] "For all that is in the world is the concupiscence of the flesh, and the concupiscence of the eyes, and the pride of life" (1 Jn 2:16).

the grace to well understand these rules of truth and holiness, in which Your law is summed up; make me to meditate upon them unceasingly, and to practice them always. O my Savior, Your Heart is thus my rule par excellence; the more that I conform myself to it, the more will the peace of God and His mercy rest upon me.[1]

XXIX

On the ineffable meekness of the Heart of Jesus Christ

Who does not recall the truly heavenly words that fell one day from Jesus's lips, or rather from His divine Heart, when, in a transport of love, He exclaimed: *"I confess to Thee, O Father, Lord of heaven and earth, because Thou hast hid these things from the wise and prudent and hast revealed them to little ones. Yea, Father, for so hath it seemed good in Thy sight.... Come to Me, all you that labour and are burdened, and I will refresh you. Take up My yoke upon you and learn of Me, because I am meek, and humble of heart: and you shall find rest to your souls. For My yoke is sweet and My burden light"* (Mt 11:25-30).

What words! They reveal to us in two words the entire secret of predestination, true holiness, true consolation, and pure happiness. How is this? By revealing to us the two principal states of the Sacred Heart of Jesus: *meekness and humility.*

---

[1] "And whosoever shall follow this rule, peace on them, and mercy, and upon the Israel of God" (Gal 6:16).

To learn this double secret, one must be simple of spirit, simple of heart. To attain this divine and blessed peace, one must go draw from its source, in the Heart of Jesus, from which both meekness and humility pour out.

First of all, what is meekness? The meekness of Jesus, which must become our meekness, is a state full of strength and sweetness, which establishes the soul in a profound and tranquil love towards God, in a most peaceful and most benevolent charity towards one's neighbor, especially amidst contradictions; and finally, in a most pure and most profound peace in relation to oneself.

Meekness is the perfection of kindness, mercy, and charity. It is the delicious oil that flows from the opened Heart of Jesus, and which comes to insinuate itself in all the faculties of our soul, mingling with our thoughts, our judgments, our words, our affections, and our daily works, big and small, to diffuse there a certain heavenly peace, a certain sweetness of love, and a certain joyous and sanctifying tranquil strength.

Nothing is powerful like the meekness of Jesus in our heart. It triumphs over everything; it is the mistress of hearts. *"Blessed are the meek: for they shall possess the land"* (Mt 5:4)! Here, "the land" is what is not heaven; it is what is bad or imperfect; it is rebellious wills, where Jesus does not reign. What is the means to make Him reign there? What is the means to make the will of God reign on earth as in heaven, *sicut in caelo et in terra*? The Savior Himself points it out to us: it is meekness, the holy meekness of His Sacred Heart.

Meekness is strength par excellence. All anger is weakness. The more one is meek, truly and piously meek in heart, spirit, tone, and language, the more one is strong. Meekness is the great weapon of Christians, amidst their tribulations and amidst the world's contradictions. It tempers our joys, thereby keeping us in an atmosphere of peace and holiness, and preserving us from dissipation. It tempers and sanctifies our indignation in the presence of evil and of the wicked, keeping us from any bitterness, passion, or human and disordered sentiment. It sweetens our tears, which are naturally so bitter.

Meekness elevates us and maintains us in the superhuman atmosphere of that "peace of God" St. Paul talks about, "which surpasses all understanding, keeping [our] hearts and minds in Christ Jesus" (Phil 4:7). It is deep, simultaneously serious and joyful, powerful and tranquil, like the blue in the sky.

This beautiful and sweet meekness, which emanated from the Heart of Jesus like light and warmth emanate from the sun, imbued all the Savior's thoughts, all His words, and all His actions. Even when He was indignant at the Pharisees, He still preserved this heavenly character of peace and meekness. Our indignation at ourselves, even when it is most legitimate, is too often imprinted with an acrid and bitter zeal. Jesus's indignation was not like that, because it came from His divinely and perfectly meek Heart.

O meekness of the Heart of the Infant Jesus, which only answers Bethlehem's ingratitude and Herod's persecutions with tears and blessings!

O meekness of the Heart of Jesus in Nazareth, which, in the humiliation of work and in the privations of poverty, unceasingly sanctifies Mary and Joseph, causes the angels to be in admiration, and gives to us all the example of true holiness!

O meekness of the Heart of Jesus! How it made Him tolerate, for three and a half years, the coarseness of His apostles and disciples, who did not yet understand anything of His doctrine, to whom it was necessary to explain everything a thousand times, to repeat everything, and who after that seemed to understand no better than before! How it makes Him tolerate Judas, the traitor and sacrilegious man! *"Friend, whereto art thou come?... Dost thou betray the Son of man with a kiss?"* (Mt 26:50; Lk 22:48). How it accompanies Him in His Holy Passion! Not one word that does not exude mildness, kindness, and peace, whether before Caiphas, whether before Pilate and Herod, or whether before the executioners, the blasphemers on Calvary, and the thieves crucified beside Him who insult Him. *"Father, forgive them, for they know not what they do"*—such is the cry of His Heart. This cry was so meek, so penetrating, that it converted the good thief.

Dear and holy meekness of the Heart of my Jesus! Oh, from now on reign supreme over all my life. Transform me; change me. Like oil in the machinery of a difficult lock, Your meekness will temper the difficulties of my character; it will make You reign over my first movements, and truly make You master of my will and my sentiments. It will bear its imprint and Your heavenly resemblance even on my face, on my physiognomy, and on all my exterior.

And it is then, only then, O Most Blessed Virgin, that you will recognize me as your true child. You will see in me your dear Jesus, charitable, benevolent, and meek and humble of heart.

XXX

On the most profound humility of the divine Heart of Jesus

"Learn of Me, because I am meek and humble of heart." Jesus is not only meek of heart, *mitis corde*; He is also humble of heart, *humilis corde*, as perfectly humble as He is perfectly meek.

We can understand the perfection of this holy humility by first considering the abasement of His Heart in the face of the infinite greatness and holiness of God; then, His sentiments with regard to the honors and glory of the world; then, finally, His sentiments with regard to humiliations, insults, and scorn.

The holy humanity of the Son of God never lost sight of God's infinite greatness which gave it existence and life, on which it totally depended, without which it had nothing and was nothing. This clear sight of its nothingness as a creature and of the everything of God its Creator, to Whom it was hypostatically united, kept it in an incomparable humility. Indeed, humility consists foremost in happily recognizing that God is everything, in us and outside of us, and that of ourselves we have nothing and are nothing. "I am the One Who is, and you are the one who is not," Jesus said one day to St. Catherine of Siena. This truth is the foundation for adoration.

The holy Heart of Jesus never forgot this. He was before God as one who is not. Hence, that absolute and universal submission; hence, that unceasing adoration, those praises, that total abandonment, and those ineffable duties of a most perfect religion. Moreover, since the Savior, despite His infinite innocence, had taken upon Himself all the sins of all sinners[1] in order to obtain forgiveness for them and to expiate them Himself, He always saw Himself before the justice of God as under sin, as the universal sinner. St. Paul says that Jesus was made sin and a "curse" on our behalf (Gal 3:13). What sin is before God, Jesus was in His own eyes. Thus, Son of God though He was, "Christ did not please Himself" (Rom 15:3). Ever abased in His Heart before first the majesty and then the holiness of God, He was as perfectly humble as He was perfectly holy. *"Learn of Me, because I am meek and humble of heart."*

O Jesus, what an example! What a lesson! And I, a true sinner and miserable, would still dare to give myself over to delusions of vain complacency! Oh, no, never again, my divine Master! I want like You, with You, and for You, to remain in the truth; I will no longer let myself be seduced by the father of the proud, who did not know how to stand in the truth, *"in veritate non stetit"* (Jn 8:44). With Your grace, I will never more forget that of myself I am nothing, nothing but a most miserable sinner; and the cry of my heart from now on will be that of the publican in the Gospel: "O God, be merciful to me a sinner" (Lk 18:13).

The second sign and at the same time the second effect of the most profound humility of the Heart of Jesus is the absolute repulsion for the esteem and glory of the world. Glory was certainly due to Him, for He is God, in union with the Father and the Holy Ghost; and when at the

---

[1] "Peccata nostra sua esse voluit" (St. Augustine).

second coming He appears to the world in all majesty and glory, angels and men will adore Him, with their faces to the ground. Yes; however, in His first coming, He came to kill the pride which killed man; and, reserving for later the radiance of His divinity, He simply shows us, in His mortal life, what sinful man is, what he must do, what he must want, and what he must flee to "stand in the truth."

Hence, rendering to God what belongs to God alone, honor, esteem, sovereignty, the majesty of glory and praise, His holy humanity rejected all this as not being due to nothingness or to the sinner. If at times, as on Mount Tabor, on Palm Sunday, and after His principal miracles, He tolerates a certain splendor around His person, it is not for Himself, but for us; it is to fortify our faith; and in this splendor, His charitable humility is only more glowing.

Before Jesus, so humble of heart, what become of my miserable pretensions to esteem and praise? Of my thirst for compliments, vainglory, and success? Of my aspirations to shine and to be applauded? Of my ambitious desires and all this absurd train of delusions and vanities, all daughters of pride? Humble and meek Jesus, teach me humility, and turn away my poor heart from perverse inclinations to vainglory.

Finally, the humility of the Sacred Heart of Jesus is manifested to us through the love that justice and truth inspired in Him for silence, for the obscure and hidden life, and for humiliations, insults, and all the abasements shining around His birth and His death.

Remember, for the love of God, the abasements of all kinds that our most adorable Savior willed to undergo in His Incarnation, when His infinite greatness shrank

Himself to the form of a poor little infant, of a humble little slave, enclosed in the womb of His creature, receiving from her life and growth; in His birth, amidst poverty and misery; throughout His childhood, which was persecuted, exiled, and as though trampled upon by men; in His adolescence, and in that long obscurity in Nazareth, all spent in coarse work and in the humblest silence; in His public life, in His penance in the desert, and in His fasts, which were accompanied by the humiliating calumnies and persecutions from the Jews; and finally, in His sorrowful Passion, where He saw Himself crushed by demons and by men, buffeted, covered with spittle, treated like a blasphemer and a crazy man, jeered at by all His people, condemned to death, and hung like a criminal. What humiliations! What unfathomable depths of abasement! And He was God!

His adorable Heart happily accepted them, because they were due to the universal sinner, to the sinner of sinners. My sins deserved all these blows; and He bore my sins.

O Jesus! And in Your tomb, where You were no longer but a corpse! And in Your Eucharist, where, veiling Your eternal splendor beneath the species of the sacrament, You have made Yourself so little for me and have exposed Yourself to all the sacrileges and outrages which have defiled Your Tabernacle for eighteen centuries! And in Your Church, so unrecognized! And in Your martyrs, and in Your members, hated and persecuted! What abasements! However, Jesus willed them all, and loved them all.

And I, a sinner; I, who dread them like fire, who flee them with all the forces of my self-love and blindness!

How different, then, is my heart from the Heart of my divine Master, willingly and joyfully assaulted by ignominies, which were repairing the dishonor done to His Father by my sins, which were delivering me from the eternal confusions of hell, which were meriting for me the glories of Paradise, which were the divine and all-powerful remedy for my detestable pride, the principle of all my sins, and which were bringing to me from heaven divine humility, the foundation of all virtues.

Heart of Jesus, model and source of humility, I adore You, love You, and consecrate myself to You forever. O most humble and most sweet Virgin Mary, obtain for me from the Sacred Heart the grace of graces, which is humility.

XXXI

How much the Heart of Jesus shows itself merciful to the little and the poor

With humility and meekness, the Heart of Jesus especially radiated mercy, tenderness, compassion, and kindness. And it was principally over children and the unfortunate that this mercy extended.

What a touching spectacle was that of the Son of God stooping with so much love to the children! Their innocence, their simplicity, and the ingenuousness of their minds and hearts delighted His divine Heart and attracted Him as though by an irresistible charm. Oh, it is that the innocent simplicity of the child is essentially but a most pure humility, unconscious of itself, as the innocence of the child is but a perfect purity which is unaware of itself and expands in joy. Jesus loved this humility and innocence above all.

Desiring one day to give His apostles a lesson in perfect humility, He called unto Him a little child, set him in the midst of them, embraced him with divine tenderness, and said to them: *"Amen I say to you, unless you be converted and become as little children, you shall not enter into the kingdom of heaven. Whosoever therefore shall humble himself as this little child, he is the greater in the kingdom of heaven. And he that shall receive one such little child in My name receiveth Me. But he that shall scandalize one of these little ones that believe in Me, it were better for him that a millstone should be hanged about his neck and that he should be drowned in the depth of the sea"* (Mt 18:3-6).

Another time, *"they brought to Him young children, that He might touch them. And the disciples rebuked them that brought them. Whom when Jesus saw, He was much displeased and saith to them: Suffer the little children to come unto Me and forbid them not; for of such is the kingdom of God.... And embracing them and laying His hands upon them, He blessed them"* (Mk 10:13-16). This is how the Son of God cherished children, showered them with His holy caresses, and enjoyed their little company.

Yes, the Heart of Jesus was for children full of sweetness, kindness, and tenderness. What He loved in them, we must love like Him and with Him; and childhood, which He loves and blesses, must be for every true Christian an object of religious respect. Holy love for children is one of the sweetest treasures of the Sacred Heart and one of the marks of the spirit of Jesus Christ. All the saints loved children.

Everyone who was little and scorned by the world, Our Lord made of them a special object of His merciful tenderness. The poor, the afflicted, the infirm, the sick, the unfortunate, in one word all those who suffer, He specially loved them. He wants us to love them as He does, for love of Him. Sympathetic to their troubles, He desires that we do good to them. His divine Heart, which has become our heart, overflows for them with a charity that is as ardent as it is tender, as strong as it is sweet. We would not belong to Jesus Christ if we were harsh with the poor, if we pushed away those He loves.

O my most good Savior, yes, I want to resemble You in this tender mercy for little ones, children, and the unfortunate. The world scorns them like it scorns You Yourself, and this is exactly why I, Your disciple, who am not of the world, want to love them as I love You, and to do good to You in their persons.

You tell us in Your holy Gospel, *"Amen I say to you, as long as you did it to one of these My least brethren, you did it to Me"* (Mt 25:40). Oh, what a wonderful rule! And what a light for my conduct with regard to children, poor orphans, the abandoned, the unfortunate, the afflicted, and all those who have recourse to me in their troubles! Woe to me if my heart is not for them the most good and most sweet Heart of Jesus! Woe to me if I mistreat my God, or if even I grieve Him through my own fault, in the person of the least of these little ones.

O adorable Heart, source of goodness, deign to fill my heart with Your goodness and tenderness, as You filled the hearts of Your saints.

XXXII

That the Immaculate Heart of Mary is but one with the most adorable Heart of Jesus

By the *Heart* of Mary, one must understand the physical Heart of her body, the spiritual Heart of her soul, and what one could call her divine Heart, meaning eternal and substantial Love, the Holy Ghost, with Whom the Blessed Virgin has been totally and divinely filled.

From this triple point of view, the Immaculate Heart of Mary belongs entirely to Jesus and has such close and indissoluble relations with the Heart of the Son of God, that this union consummates both in a kind of oneness, *consummati in unum.*

The physical Heart of Jesus comes entirely from the virginal Heart of His Mother, who alone provided the Incarnate Word the substance of His humanity, and consequently the substance of the noblest and foremost organ of this adorable humanity, which is His Heart. Faith teaches us that when the heavenly Father begot in time, in the Virgin's womb, Him Whom He begets eternally in heaven, the Holy Ghost, Who is the Spirit of love and union, worked this ineffable mystery of the Incarnation of the Word by taking the purest flower of Mary's immaculate blood to form Jesus's adorable body. Now, as everyone knows, blood and the heart are but one in the human body: the heart is the principle and source of blood; the heart sends blood to all the members to give them life, and the blood faithfully returns to the heart as its first principle, to again be sent and given to the body. The divine Heart of the Infant Jesus was thus formed entirely from the very substance and the single substance of the Virgin, His Mother; if it is the work of the Holy Ghost, it is also the work of Mary; and it belongs entirely to its Mother, as well as to its divine Father. If St. Augustine could and did say, "The flesh of Christ is the flesh of Mary, *caro Christi, caro Mariae*," it is no less true to say, not due to a confusion, but by virtue of an intimate union: "The Heart of Jesus is the Heart of Mary, and the Heart of Mary is the Heart of Jesus."

The spiritual Heart of Mary and the Sacred Heart of Jesus are also but one heart, due to an indissoluble union of mind, will, sentiments, and affections. If it is said of the first Christians that they had but one heart and one soul, "*cor unum et anima una*" (Acts 4:32), how much more can and must it be said of the only Son of Mary and of His most holy, most dear Mother?

If St. Bernard could say that since Jesus is his head, the Heart of Jesus is his heart, and that in this way he has truly but one same heart with Jesus, "*ego vere cum Jesu cor unum habeo,*"[1] how much more truthfully can Immaculate Mary Most Holy say, "The Heart of my head and of my Son is my heart, and I have but one heart with Him"?

Thus, she one day told her dear daughter and servant St. Bridget: "*Know that I loved my Son so ardently and that He loved me so tenderly that He and I were as but one heart; quasi cor unum ambo fuimus.*"

She added, "*My Son was truly like my Heart to me: when He suffered, it was as if my Heart was enduring His*

---

[1] *Tractatus de passione Domini, super istud Joannis: Ego sum vitis vera*, ch. 3.

torments and pains. His sorrow was my sorrow, and His Heart was my Heart."

And Our Lord for His part taught the same thing to the same St. Bridget, when, appearing to her one day and conversing familiarly with her, He said to her: "*I Who am God and Son of God from all eternity, I made Myself man in the womb of the Virgin, whose Heart was as My Heart—this is why My Mother and I have worked man's salvation with one same Heart so to speak, quasi cum uno corde.*"

Thus, the spiritual Heart of the Most Blessed Virgin and her immaculate, impeccable, most perfectly holy, humble, meek, and obedient soul were but one with the Heart and the soul of her adorable Son.

Finally, it must be said with more absolute precision that the divine and eternal Heart of Jesus, which is the Spirit of love and Love itself, was truly the divine Heart of Mary and the single principle of her life, her thoughts, her affections, and all her movements.

The Holy Ghost, Who is in us the Spirit of Jesus Christ, *Spiritus Christi* (Rom 8:9), was so in fullness in the soul of the Most Blessed Virgin. He united her in such a perfect and divine manner to Jesus, and through Jesus to the heavenly Father, that this union, which is the grace, joy, and crown of the Mother of God, is an unfathomable mystery, whose holy depths God alone can fathom, and in which St. Bonaventure saw "something infinite."

Thus, the Heart of Jesus and the Heart of Mary are but one in the Holy Ghost. Oh, may they also be but one in our love and in our homage!

Yes, Jesus is the heart and life of His Blessed Mother. He communicates to her His divine life with such superabundance that it is impossible to even compare this life of Jesus in Mary with the life of Jesus in His greatest saints and in His most sublime angels. St. Paul exclaimed, "*I live, now not I; but Christ liveth in me*" (Gal 2:20).

"I live," tells us from the height of heaven the Queen of Angels and Saints, the Mother of Life, the all heavenly Mother of God; "I live, but it is not I; it is Jesus, it is my Son, my Lord, and my Savior Who lives in me. He is living in my soul; He is living in my body; He is living in all the faculties of my soul and body."

Jesus is fully living in Mary, meaning everything in Jesus that is communicable is living in Mary: His Heart is living in her Heart; His soul in her soul; and His mind in her mind.

"*What therefore God hath joined together*," Our Lord says, "*let no man put asunder*" (Mt 19:6). In His divine plan, God having intimately joined together Jesus and Mary, the Heart of the Son and the Heart of the Mother, let no one separate them in his own heart. In adoring the Heart of Jesus, let us venerate and bless the Heart of Mary; and in rendering this cult of *hyperdulia*, meaning *super-veneration*, to the Most Holy and Immaculate Heart of the Mother of God, let us render to the Divine and Most Sacred Heart of her Son the cult of *latria*, meaning actual adoration, which heaven and earth owe Him. In heaven, we shall eternally continue this double cult with the angels and the blessed. Oh, how good it will be to bless Jesus and Mary up above, to contemplate them face to face, to feel our hearts on their Hearts, and to inebriate ourselves with their holy love!

O Most Sacred Heart of Jesus, have mercy on us! *Cor Jesu sacratissimum, miserere nobis!*

O Immaculate Heart of Mary, pray for us! *Cor Mariae immaculatum, ora pro nobis!*

XXXIII

The Sacred Heart of Jesus and France[1]

In the magnificent revelations to Blessed Margaret Mary, there is the issue of France's destiny, and the special tribute of adoration France will have to render to the Heart of Jesus.

On 17 June 1689, the Blessed Sister wrote, "The Divine Heart desires to magnificently enter the houses of princes and kings, to be honored there as much as He was insulted, scorned, and humiliated in His Passion. He must have as much joy in seeing the great ones of the earth humbled before Him, as He felt bitterness in seeing Himself annihilated at their feet.

"And these are the words I heard in this regard: '*Make known to the Eldest Son of My Sacred Heart that he will obtain his birth of eternal glory through his consecration to My adorable Heart. My Heart desires to triumph over his, and, through his mediation, the hearts of the great ones of the earth.*'

"'*My Heart desires to reign in the palace of the King of France, to be painted on his standards and engraved*

---

[1] For the closing day of the month of the Sacred Heart, the pious reader will forgive me for offering him a bit longer of a reading. The subject on which we are going to rest our hopes and our hearts is so exciting, so full of relevance today, and so practical that surely no one will think to complain.

on his weapons, in order to render them victorious over all his enemies, and over all the enemies of the Holy Church.'"

Jesus Himself calls the King of France *"the Eldest Son of His Sacred Heart."* What a name! What a title! To what other prince has the divine munificence ever conferred this? And what an honor for France herself!

What Jesus is asking here of the King of France, none of our princes has yet sufficiently understood it. Let us ask the Heart of Jesus to soon give us the true Eldest Son of the Sacred Heart, a truly *most Christian* King.

In the month of August of the same year 1689, Blessed Margaret Mary returned to the same subject. "The Eternal Father means to make use of the King of France to have built a temple where would be placed the image of the Divine Heart of His Son, in order to receive there the consecration and homage of the King and of the entire Court.

"Additionally, this Divine Heart wants to make itself the protector and defender of his sacred person against all his visible and invisible enemies. It has chosen him as his faithful friend, to obtain from the Apostolic Holy See the privileges that must accompany devotion to this Divine Heart. It is through the Heart of Jesus that He will accord him the treasures of His graces and pour His blessings over all his undertakings."

Alas, what account have our kings taken of these magnificent and consoling promises? God knows whether a greater fidelity would have spared France the scandals of the eighteenth century and the terrible catastrophes which were their consequence and punishment.

The pious Queen Marie Leszczyńska, the wife of Louis XV, better understood the Savior's wish. In 1765, she obtained from the General Assembly of the Clergy of France that public veneration and the Mass and Office of the Sacred Heart be officially established in all the dioceses of the kingdom; but it was to the King, not to the Queen, that the Son of God had appealed; and at that time still, whilst allowing everything, the King of France had done nothing. As the King had not taken part as King, France had not taken part as a nation; Our Savior wanted more.

Finally, in 1792, the unfortunate Louis XVI, a prisoner in the Tuileries, under the watch, or rather in the clutches of the Revolutionary Convention, which was soon going to kill him, made this act of consecration, asked for more than a century prior. Alas, it was too late, perhaps not for France, but for the King of France.

It was in the first months of that fatal year that Louis XVI consecrated France to the Sacred Heart, under the inspiration of Fr. Eudes' pious successor, Fr. Hébert, martyred at Les Carmes Prison on the following 2 September. These are the very words of the King-Martyr's vow:

"You see, O my God, all the wounds that tear my heart, and the depth of the abyss into which I have fallen. Countless evils surround me from all sides. To my own and my family's misfortunes, which are dreadful, are joined, to overwhelm my soul, the misfortunes which cover the face of the kingdom. The cries of all the unfortunate and the groanings of oppressed religion resound in my ears, and an interior voice further warns me that perhaps Your justice faults me for all these calamities, because in the days of my power I did not suppress the license of the people and irreligion, which are their principal sources; because I myself provided weapons to the heresy that triumphs, by favoring it through laws which doubled its powers and gave it the boldness to dare everything.

"I will not have the temerity, O my God, to justify myself before You; but You know that my heart has always been subject to the faith and to the rules of morals; my faults are the fruit of my weakness and seem worthy of Your great mercy. You forgave King David, who had caused Your enemies to blaspheme against You; and King Manasses, who had led his people into idolatry. Disarmed by their penitence, You reestablished both of them on the throne of Judah; You had them reign with peace and glory. Would You today be unmoved for a son of St. Louis, who takes these penitent kings as models and who, after their example, desires to repair his faults and become a King according to Your Heart?

"O Jesus Christ, Divine Redeemer of all our iniquities, it is in Your adorable Heart that I wish to place the outpourings of my afflicted soul. I call to my help the tender Heart of Mary, my august protectress and my Mother, and the assistance of St. Louis, my Patron and the most illustrious of my ancestors.

"Open, adorable Heart, and through the such pure hands of my powerful intercessors, receive with kindness the expiatory vows that confidence inspires in me, and that I offer You as the simple expression of my sentiments.

"If, by an effect of God's infinite goodness, I regain my liberty, my crown, and my royal power, I solemnly promise:

"1. To revoke as soon as possible all those laws, including the Civil Constitution of the Clergy, that will be designated to me by the Pope, a Council, or four bishops chosen amongst the most enlightened and virtuous in my kingdom, as being contrary to the purity and integrity of the faith and to the discipline and spiritual jurisdiction of the Holy, Catholic, Apostolic, and Roman Church;

"2. To take, within the span of one year, with both the Pope and the Bishops of my kingdom, all the measures necessary to establish, in accordance with canonical forms, a solemn feast in honor of the Sacred Heart of Jesus, which will be celebrated in perpetuity in all of France on the first Friday after the octave of Corpus Christi, and always followed by a general procession in reparation for the outrages and profanations committed in our holy temples during the time of troubles by schismatics, heretics, and bad Christians;

"3. To go in person myself, within three months from the day of my liberation, into the church of Notre-Dame de Paris, or into any other principal church in the place where I am, and to pronounce on a Sunday or feast day, at the foot of the main altar after the offertory of the Mass, and between the hands of the celebrant, a solemn act of consecration of my person, of my family, and of my kingdom to the Sacred Heart of Jesus with the promise to give all my subjects the example of veneration and devotion due to this adorable Heart.

"4. To erect and decorate at my own expense, in the church that I will choose for this, within one year from the day of my liberation, a chapel or an altar that would be dedicated to the Sacred Heart of Jesus, and which will serve as a perpetual memorial of my gratitude and boundless confidence in the infinite merits and inexhaustible treasures of graces enclosed in this Sacred Heart.

"5. Finally, to renew each year, at the place I happen to be on the day that the feast of the Sacred Heart will be celebrated, the act of consecration expressed in the third article, and to assist in the general procession that follows the Mass of this day.

"Today I can only secretly pronounce this promise, but I would sign it in my blood were it necessary; and the most beautiful day of my life will be the one when I can publicize it aloud in the temple.

"O ADORABLE HEART OF MY SAVIOR! Let me forget my right hand and let me forget my very self, if ever I forget Your benefits and my promises, if I cease to love You and to place in You my confidence and all my consolation. Amen."

This cry of prayer and of distress did not have its full effect. Why? Perhaps because Louis XVI was no longer king but in name when he made this solemn promise. God wants France to be consecrated to the Heart of Jesus by her real Sovereign acting as Sovereign! At least the pious monarch drew from this divine source the heroism of martyrdom; and his appeal did not remain without echo. Shortly afterwards, the Vendée rose up, and we know well that "this race of giants," the Bonchamps, the Cathelineaus, the Lescures, the La Rochejacqueleins, and all the others, gentlemen and peasants, prided themselves on going into battle with the image of the Sacred Heart on their chests!

The [Bourbon] Restoration [from 1814 to 1830], despite the very sincere piety of the royal family, did not do what Our Lord had requested. Something was done, certainly; but not everything was done; the promises of Louis XVI were not kept.

Jesus repeatedly complained of this to a very holy religious sister of the Congregation of Notre Dame, who lived at the time at Les Oiseaux Convent on Rue de Sèvres in Paris. This holy girl, whose religious name was Sister Mary of Jesus, was on fire with love for the Divine Heart and lived for this Heart alone:

"Immersed in an ocean of light," writes the venerable Fr. Ronsin, her confessor, "she clearly saw there the desires of this adorable Heart all aflame with love for men, and the special designs of mercy for France. It was said to her and often repeated by Jesus Christ Himself, in her ecstasies, that the vow of France's consecration to the Sacred Heart, attributed to Louis XVI, was truly made by him; that it was he who had written and pronounced it. *The divine Savior had added that He ardently desired that this vow be executed, meaning that the King consecrate his family and his entire kingdom to the Sacred Heart, as Louis XIII had done before to the Blessed Virgin; that he have its feast solemnly and universally celebrated every year on the Friday after the octave of Corpus Christi; and lastly, that he have built a chapel and erect an altar in its honor.*" On this condition, the Divine Savior *promised the most abundant blessings for the King, the royal family, and all of France.*

On 21 June 1823, these revelations were repeated with greater clarity. She was told in formal terms: "FRANCE IS STILL VERY DEAR TO MY DIVINE HEART, AND SHE WILL BE CONSECRATED TO IT. BUT IT MUST BE THE KING HIMSELF WHO CONSECRATES HIS PERSON, HIS FAMILY, AND HIS ENTIRE KINGDOM TO MY DIVINE HEART; *and that he, as I have already said, have an altar erected to it, just as one was erected in the name of France in honor of the Blessed Virgin.* I AM PREPARING FOR FRANCE A DELUGE OF GRACES FOR WHEN SHE IS CONSECRATED TO MY DIVINE HEART." – Our Lord continued: *"How is this? The outrages committed against the royal majesty have been publicly repaired, whilst the countless outrages I have received in the sacrament of My love have not yet been repaired! One fears to speak to the King; one fears he is not disposed to hear about this double happiness for him, as well as for his family and for his kingdom! Oh, I hold all hearts in My hand, and the heart of the King is disposed to do everything that will be asked of him for My glory. Every day he gives proofs of this. The request made of him to work for the beatification of Mother Margaret Mary Alacoque, was it not perfectly received? Let N*** speak, and he will see.* I AM PREPARING EVERYTHING: FRANCE WILL BE CONSECRATED TO MY DIVINE HEART, AND ALL THE EARTH WILL FEEL THE EFFECTS OF THE BLESSINGS I POUR OUT UPON HER. FAITH AND RELIGION WILL FLOURISH AGAIN IN FRANCE THROUGH DEVOTION TO MY DIVINE HEART."

We hoped a moment would come for the solemn fulfillment of Louis XVI's vow through the mediation of his august and holy daughter. But the events of 1830 again postponed the saving project.

The cult of the Heart of Jesus had not ceased to develop in the hearts of the pious faithful, among members of the clergy, and especially within religious communities.

Around 1840, an admirable work was born, the work of the Apostolate of Prayer, which is nothing other than the league of Christian hearts united to the Heart of Jesus for the triumph of the Church and the salvation of souls. This association, for which France was the birthplace, today encompasses the world and counts members in the millions.

It is therefore not surprising that in 1870, at the time of unprecedented disasters for our France, believers turned their eyes towards this adorable Heart, from which must come our salvation. A vow was formulated by a great number of faithful, with the goal of at last preparing the fulfillment of Louis XVI's vow. Here is the text:

"In the presence of the misfortunes which are desolating France, of the greater misfortunes perhaps which threaten her still;

"In the presence of the sacrilegious assaults committed in Rome against the rights of the Church and of the Holy See, and against the sacred person of the Vicar of Jesus Christ;

"All whilst acknowledging that our unfortunate homeland has deserved God's chastisements through the scandals for which it has been the theatre, through the encouragements it has given to the revolutionary spirit in the world, and in particular through the guilty abandonment of the cause of the Sovereign Pontiff and of the Church, an abandonment which has only too easily been accepted;

"To make amends for our sins, to receive forgiveness for them through the merciful intervention of the Sacred Heart of Our Lord Jesus Christ, and to obtain, through the same intervention, the extraordinary helps which alone can deliver the Sovereign Pontiff, make France's misfortunes cease, and bring religious and societal renewal, we promise, when these graces will have been granted, to contribute, according to our means, to erect in Paris a church consecrated to the Sacred Heart of Jesus, the erecting of which will be requested of the competent ecclesiastical authority."

At the same time that this noble idea was spreading like fire everywhere, the honor of the French armies, so sadly compromised in our recent battles, was finding an inviolable refuge in the hearts of de Charette's and Cathelineau's intrepid volunteers. These brave men, returning to the great traditions of the first Vendée, followed into combat the rejuvenated standard of the Sacred Heart, which they crimsoned with their generous blood in the fields of Loigny and Le Mans; and, owing to the power of the faith, "the Pope's soldiers" were the best soldiers in France.

One day, in Rennes (it was Saturday and the Vigil of Pentecost, the same time that the Commune's execrable reign in Paris was ending), these valiant defenders of the Holy See and of France solemnly consecrated themselves to the Sacred Heart of Jesus.

It was a sublime spectacle. The brave General de Charette, barely recovered from his injuries, surrounded by his glorious companions in arms, and standing before the holy altar next to the flag displayed by the Zouaves, on which was embroidered the Sacred Heart crowned with thorns and surrounded with the legend *Heart of Jesus, save France!*, read aloud this act of consecration. He had just received it from the most Christian and most valiant General de Sonis, kept far away by the effects of a thousand-times glorious amputation. The words were as follows:

"O Jesus, true Son of God, our King and our Brother, gathered here at the foot of Your altars, we come to fully give ourselves to You and to consecrate ourselves to Your Divine Heart.

"You know, Lord, we have armed ourselves for the defense of the holiest of causes, of Your cause, Lord, since we are the soldiers of Your Vicar.

"You have permitted us to be associated with the sorrows of Pius IX, and after having shared his humiliations to be violently separated from our Father.

"Yet, Lord, after having been driven from that Roman land where we stood guard at the tomb of the Holy Apostles, You prepared other duties for us, and You allowed 'the Pope's soldiers' to become 'France's soldiers.'

"We showed up at the battlefields, armed to fight. Your adorable Heart, depicted on our flag, sheltered our battalions.

"Lord, France's land has drunk our blood, and You know if we have well made the sacrifice of our life to the homeland.

"Many of our brothers have died; You called them back to Yourself because they were ripe for heaven.

"But we ourselves remain, and we do not know the fate You have reserved for us.

"My God, let the life You have left us be entirely consecrated to Your service.

"We bear on our chests the image of Your Sacred Heart; let our own hearts be even truer images of it; make us worthy of the title of Christian soldiers.

"Make us subject to our leaders, charitable to our neighbors, strict with ourselves, devoted to our duties, and ready for all sacrifices.

"Make us pure in body and soul, that ardent in combat, we become tender and compassionate towards the wounded.

"O Jesus, in dangers and sufferings, it is from Your Divine Heart that we expect our most powerful help. It will be our refuge when all human support fails us, and our last breath will be our last act of hope in infinite mercy.

"And you, O divine Mary, whom we have chosen for our Mother, to you also we have borne witness.

"Our battlefields have seen the long train of mothers, wives, and sisters in mourning; and when pious hands moved the earth that covered death, one knew how to recognize our own through your scapular.

"Be then our protectress and obtain for us the grace to keep ourselves Christianly united to you in the Sacred Heart of Jesus, during life and at death, for time and for eternity. Amen."

And General de Charette, looking at and showing the flag of the Sacred Heart stained with the blood of his Zouaves, said in a calm, clear, and strongly accented voice:

"In the shadow of this flag, stained with the blood of our noblest and dearest casualties, I, Baron General de Charette, who have the distinguished honor of commanding you, consecrate the Legion of the Volunteers of the West, the Papal Zouaves, to the Sacred Heart of Jesus; and, with my soldier's faith, I say with all my soul, and ask all of you to say it with me: HEART OF JESUS, SAVE FRANCE!!!"

And everyone, of one heart and in a single voice, uttered the cry of the homeland's salvation: HEART OF JESUS, SAVE FRANCE!

On the day when all of France will repeat it, the day when the most Christian king, the grandson of St. Louis will repeat it before heaven and earth, obeying at last the merciful orders of the King of kings, France will be saved, and, through France, Rome and the Church!

Adorable Heart of Jesus, make shine as soon as possible that great and beautiful day.

Prayers

The invocations in the following beautiful litanies of the Most Sacred Heart of Jesus and of the Immaculate Heart of Mary have been extracted, through the efforts of the venerable Father Eudes, from Holy Scripture, the Fathers and Doctors of the Church, as well as writings of the Saints. They have been canonically approved by many bishops.

I would encourage pious persons who would use the Litanies of the Holy Heart of Mary for the practice of the month of the Sacred Heart to recite one day the first one and the following day the second one, alternating them in this way for the entire month. They are so pious and so beautiful that it would truly be a pity to lose something of them.

To persons who would do this daily exercise in common, I would dare to recommend a very devout method for reciting the litanies in general, and these in particular: Instead of just responding *Have mercy on us* or *Pray for us* at each invocation recited by the person presiding over the exercise, it would be better to alternate, as is done for the Psalms. The one who presides says the first invocation with the response; the others present say the second invocation, also with the response, and so forth until the end.

Nothing is so simple and pious as this way of praying, so commonly used in the Church. The very simple prayer, expressed by the *Have mercy on us* or the *Pray for us*, which crowns all the invocations in the litanies, is the cry of the humble and confident soul at the feet of Jesus and Mary.

LITANY OF THE SACRED HEART OF JESUS
taken from Father Eudes[1]

Kyrie, eleison.	Lord, have mercy on us.
Christe, eleison.	Christ, have mercy on us.
Kyrie, eleison.	Lord, have mercy on us.
Jesu, audi nos.	Jesus, hear us.
Jesu, exaudi nos.	Jesus, graciously hear us.
Pater de caelis Deus, *miserere nobis.*	God the Father of Heaven, *have mercy on us.*
Fili, Redemptor mundi Deus, *miserere nobis.*	God the Son, Redeemer of the world, *have mercy on us.*
Spiritus Sancte Deus, *miserere nobis.*	God the Holy Ghost, *have mercy on us.*
Sancta Trinitas unus Deus, *miserere nobis.*	Holy Trinity, one God, *have mercy on us.*
Cor Jesu sacratissimum, *miserere nobis.*	Most Sacred Heart of Jesus, *have mercy on us.*
Cor Jesu divinissimum, *etc.*	Heart of Jesus most divine, *etc.*
Cor Jesu adorandum,	Heart of Jesus to be adored,
Cor Jesu amantissimum,	Heart of Jesus most loving,
Cor Jesu mitissimum,	Heart of Jesus most meek,
Cor Jesu humillimum,	Heart of Jesus most humble,
Cor Jesu misericordissimum,	Heart of Jesus most merciful,

---

[1] This version of the Litany of the Sacred Heart is a reproduction of that found in the original 1872 French version of this book. The reader should be aware that it is different from the standard version the Church approved in 1899 for public use.—Trans.

Cor Jesu, plenitudo divinitatis,	Heart of Jesus, fullness of the Godhead,
Cor Jesu, sanctuarium Trinitatis,	Heart of Jesus, sanctuary of the Trinity,
Cor Jesu, thronus divinae voluntatis,	Heart of Jesus, throne of the Divine Will,
Cor Jesu, fornax amoris,	Heart of Jesus, furnace of love,
Cor Jesu, miraculum sanctitatis,	Heart of Jesus, marvel of holiness,
Cor Jesu, exemplar omnium virtutum,	Heart of Jesus, model of all virtues,
Cor Jesu, fons omnium gratiarum,	Heart of Jesus, fountain of all graces,
Cor Jesu, amore vulneratum,	Heart of Jesus, wounded by love,
Cor Jesu, dolore disruptum,	Heart of Jesus, broken by pain,
Cor Jesu, lancea transfixum,	Heart of Jesus, pierced with a lance,
Cor Jesu, templum charitatis,	Heart of Jesus, temple of charity,
Cor Jesu, altare dilectionis,	Heart of Jesus, altar of love,
Cor Jesu, thuribulum aureum,	Heart of Jesus, golden censer,
Cor Jesu, holocaustum aeternum,	Heart of Jesus, eternal holocaust,
Cor Jesu, calix inebrians,	Heart of Jesus, inebriating chalice,
Cor Jesu, consolatio afflictorum,	Heart of Jesus, consolation of the afflicted,
Cor Jesu, refugium peccatorum,	Heart of Jesus, refuge of sinners,

Cor Jesu, pax nostra charissima,	Heart of Jesus, our dearest peace,
Cor Jesu, spes nostra dulcissima,	Heart of Jesus, our sweetest hope,
Cor Jesu, cordis nostri gaudium,	Heart of Jesus, joy of our hearts,
Cor Jesu, cordis nostri thesaurus,	Heart of Jesus, treasure of our hearts,
Cor Jesu, cordis nostri paradisus,	Heart of Jesus, paradise of our hearts,
Cor Jesu, vita cordis nostri,	Heart of Jesus, life of our hearts,
Cor Jesu, Rex cordis nostri,	Heart of Jesus, King of our hearts,
Cor Jesu, Cor Virginis Matris,	Heart of Jesus, the Heart of the Virgin Mother,
Propitius esto, *parce nobis, Jesu.*	Be merciful, *spare us, O Jesus.*
Propitius esto, *exaudi nos, Jesu.*	Be merciful, *graciously hear us, O Jesus.*
Ab omni peccato, *libera nos, Jesu.*	From all sin, *deliver us, O Jesus.*
A superbia vitae, *libera nos, Jesu.*	From the pride of life, *deliver us, O Jesus.*
Ab inordinato amore, *libera nos, Jesu.*	From disordered love, *deliver us, O Jesus.*
A caecitate cordis, *etc.*	From blindness of heart, *etc.*
A neglectu inspirationum tuarum,	From the neglect of Thine inspirations,
A morte perpetua,	From everlasting death,
Per Cor tuum amantissimum,	Through Thy most loving Heart,

Per maximum ejus in peccatum odium,	Through Its supreme hatred for sin,
Per infinitum ejus in Patrem aeternum amorem,	Through Its infinite love for the Eternal Father,
Per dulcissimam ejus in Matrem sanctissimam dilectionem,	Through Its most tender love for Thy most holy Mother,
Per summum ejus erga crucem affectum,	Through Its greatest affection for the Cross,
Per acerbissimos dolores illius,	Through Its most bitter sufferings,
Per ipsum amore et dolore in cruce disruptum,	Through that very Heart broken by love and sorrow on the Cross,
Per aeterna ejus gaudia,	Through Its eternal joys,
Agnus Dei, qui tollis peccata mundi, *parce nobis, Jesu.*	Lamb of God, Who takest away the sins of the world, *spare us, O Jesus.*
Agnus Dei, qui tollis peccata mundi, *exaudi nos, Jesu.*	Lamb of God, Who takest away the sins of the world, *graciously hear us, O Jesus.*
Agnus Dei, qui tollis peccata mundi, *miserere nobis, Jesu.*	Lamb of God, Who takest away the sins of the world, *have mercy on us, O Jesus.*
Jesu, audi nos. *Jesu, exaudi nos.*	Jesus, hear us. *Jesus, graciously hear us.*
Amen.	Amen.

LITANY OF THE HOLY HEART OF MARY
taken from Father Eudes

Kyrie, eleison.	Lord, have mercy on us.
Christe, eleison.	Christ, have mercy on us.
Kyrie, eleison.	Lord, have mercy on us.
Pater de caelis Deus, *miserere nobis.*	God the Father of Heaven, *have mercy on us.*
Fili, Redemptor mundi Deus, *miserere nobis.*	God the Son, Redeemer of the world, *have mercy on us.*
Spiritus Sancte Deus, *miserere nobis.*	God the Holy Ghost, *have mercy on us.*
Sancta Trinitas unus Deus, *miserere nobis.*	Holy Trinity, one God, *have mercy on us.*
Cor Jesu sacratissimum, *miserere nobis.*	Most Sacred Heart of Jesus, *have mercy on us.*
Cor Mariae sanctissimum, *ora pro nobis.*	Most Holy Heart of Mary, *pray for us.*
Cor Mariae, gaudium Patris aeterni, *ora pro nobis.*	Heart of Mary, joy of the Eternal Father, *pray for us.*
Cor Mariae, deliciae Filii Dei, *etc.*	Heart of Mary, delight of the Son of God, *etc.*
Cor Mariae, triumphus Spiritus Sancti,	Heart of Mary, triumph of the Holy Ghost,
Cor Mariae, regnum Sanctae Trinitatis,	Heart of Mary, kingdom of the Holy Trinity,
Cor Mariae, unum cum Corde Christi,	Heart of Mary, one with the Heart of Christ,
Cor Mariae, opus Excelsi,	Heart of Mary, masterpiece of the Most High,
Cor Mariae, requies divinitatis,	Heart of Mary, repose of the Divinity,

Cor Mariae, Deiferum,	Heart of Mary, bearer of God,
Cor Mariae, currus Jesu igneus,	Heart of Mary, chariot of fire of Jesus Christ,
Cor Mariae, hortus Sponsi virginum,	Heart of Mary, garden of the Bridegroom of virgins,
Cor Mariae, paradisus deliciarum,	Heart of Mary, paradise of delights,
Cor Mariae, reclinatorium aureum veri Salomonis,	Heart of Mary, golden resting place of the true Solomon,
Cor Mariae, cubiculum charitatis divinae,	Heart of Mary, chamber of divine charity,
Cor Mariae, verum altare Holocausti,	Heart of Mary, true altar of the Holocaust,
Cor Mariae, vas aureum plenum manna,	Heart of Mary, golden vessel full of manna,
Cor Mariae, caelum Christi,	Heart of Mary, heaven of Jesus Christ,
Cor Mariae, altare sempiterni thymiamatis,	Heart of Mary, altar of perpetual incense,
Cor Mariae, mysterium intrinsecus latens,	Heart of Mary, mystery lying hidden within,
Cor Mariae, ornamentum caeli pulcherrimum,	Heart of Mary, the most beautiful ornament of heaven,
Cor Mariae, compendium ineffabilium perfectionum Dei,	Heart of Mary, compendium of God's ineffable perfections,
Cor Mariae, custos fidelis omnium donorum Spiritus Sancti,	Heart of Mary, faithful guardian of all the gifts of the Holy Ghost,

Cor Mariae, favus mellis,	Heart of Mary, comb of honey,
Cor Mariae immaculatum,	Immaculate Heart of Mary,
Cor Mariae, forma innocentiae,	Heart of Mary, exemplar of innocence,
Cor Mariae, paradisus mansuetudinis,	Heart of Mary, paradise of meekness,
Cor Mariae, abyssus humilitatis,	Heart of Mary, unfathomable depth of humility,
Cor Mariae, templum pacis,	Heart of Mary, temple of peace,
Cor Mariae, rubus ardens et incombustus,	Heart of Mary, burning yet unburnt bush,
Cor Mariae, margarita Christi pretiosa,	Heart of Mary, precious pearl of Christ,
Cor Mariae, oraculum Ecclesiae nascentis,	Heart of Mary, oracle of the nascent Church,
Cor Mariae, solatium exilii nostri,	Heart of Mary, comfort in our exile,
Cor Mariae, fons perennis benedictionum,	Heart of Mary, ever-flowing fountain of blessings,
Cor Mariae, spes et laetitia cordis nostri,	Heart of Mary, hope and joy of our hearts,
Cor Matris Jesu dignissimum,	Most worthy Heart of the Mother of Jesus,
Cor Matris nostrae studiosissimum,	Most devoted Heart of our Mother,
Propitius esto, *parce nobis, Jesu.*	Be merciful, *spare us, O Jesus.*
Propitius esto, *exaudi nos, Jesu.*	Be merciful, *graciously hear us, O Jesus.*

Per Cor amantissimum Beatissimae Matris tuae, *exaudi nos, Jesu.*	Through the most loving Heart of Thy Most Blessed Mother, *graciously hear us, O Jesus.*
Per summum ejus in Patrem tuum amorem, *exaudi nos, Jesu.*	Through her Heart's supreme love for Thy Father, *graciously hear us, O Jesus.*
Per ardentissimam ejus in te dilectionem, *etc.*	Through her Heart's most ardent love for Thee, *etc.*
Per excellentissimam ejus cum Corde tuo unionem,	Through her Heart's most sublime union with Thine own,
Per specialem ejus erga sibi devotos charitatem,	Through her Heart's special love for those devoted to It,
Per piissima illius desideria,	Through her Heart's most pious desires,
Per omnes purissimos illius affectus,	Through all her Heart's most pure affections,
Per omnes sanctissimos illius motus,	Through all her Heart's most holy movements,
Per acerbissimos dolores ipsius,	Through her Heart's most bitter sorrows,
Per temporalia et aeterna ejus gaudia,	Through her Heart's joys in time and in eternity,
O pretiosissimum Cor Jesu et Mariae, thesaurus cordis nostri, *posside cor nostrum in aeternum.*	O most precious Hearts of Jesus and Mary, treasure of our hearts, *possess our hearts forever.*
O amantissimum Cor Jesu et Mariae, vita cordis	O most loving Hearts of Jesus and Mary, life of

nostri, *vive in corde nostro in aeternum.*	our hearts, *live in our hearts forever.*
O dilectissimum Cor Jesu et Mariae, Rex cordis nostri, *regna super cor nostrum in aeternum.*	O most beloved Hearts of Jesus and Mary, Sovereigns of our hearts, *reign over our hearts forever.*
Jesu, Cor Mariae, *audi nos.*	Jesus, Heart of Mary, *hear us.*
Jesu, Cor Mariae, *exaudi nos.*	Jesus, Heart of Mary, *graciously hear us.*
Amen.	Amen.

ANOTHER LITANY OF THE HOLY HEART OF MARY
also taken from Father Eudes

Kyrie, eleison.	Lord, have mercy on us.
Christe, eleison.	Christ, have mercy on us.
Kyrie, eleison.	Lord, have mercy on us.
Pater de caelis Deus, *miserere nobis.*	God the Father of Heaven, *have mercy on us.*
Fili, Redemptor mundi Deus, *miserere nobis.*	God the Son, Redeemer of the world, *have mercy on us.*
Spiritus Sancte Deus, *miserere nobis.*	God the Holy Ghost, *have mercy on us.*
Sancta Trinitas unus Deus, *miserere nobis.*	Holy Trinity, one God, *have mercy on us.*
Cor Jesu sacratissimum, *miserere nobis.*	Most Sacred Heart of Jesus, *have mercy on us.*

Cor Mariae sanctissimum, *ora pro nobis.*

Cor Mariae, thesaurus Patris aeterni, *ora pro nobis.*

Cor Mariae, thronus filii Dei, *etc.*

Cor Mariae, organum Spiritus Sancti,

Cor Mariae, sanctuarium divinae Trinitatis,

Cor Mariae, digna sedes Altissimi,

Cor Mariae, tabernaculum Creatoris,

Cor Mariae, basilica sacra mundi Salvatoris,

Cor Mariae, arca Testamenti,

Cor Mariae, tabula Legis digito Dei scripta,

Cor Mariae, clavis caelestis Thesauri,

Cor Mariae, radius aeternae Sanctitatis,

Cor Mariae, Cordis Christi effigies vera,

Cor Mariae, liber incomprehensus Verbi vitae,

Cor Mariae, liber vivus gestorum Christi,

Most Holy Heart of Mary, *pray for us.*

Heart of Mary, treasure of the Eternal Father, *pray for us.*

Heart of Mary, throne of the Son of God, *etc.*

Heart of Mary, instrument of the Holy Ghost,

Heart of Mary, sanctuary of the Divine Trinity,

Heart of Mary, worthy seat of the Most High,

Heart of Mary, tabernacle of the Creator,

Heart of Mary, sacred basilica of the Savior of the world,

Heart of Mary, Ark of the Covenant,

Heart of Mary, tablet of the Law written by the finger of God,

Heart of Mary, key to the Heavenly Treasury,

Heart of Mary, ray of eternal holiness,

Heart of Mary, true image of the Heart of Christ,

Heart of Mary, incomprehensible book of the Word of life,

Heart of Mary, living book of the deeds of Christ,

Cor Mariae, speculum clarissimum vitae Redemptoris,	Heart of Mary, most clear mirror of the Redeemer's life,
Cor Mariae, imago perfecta Passionis et mortis ejus,	Heart of Mary, perfect image of the Redeemer's Passion and death,
Cor Mariae, speculum divinarum perfectionum,	Heart of Mary, mirror of divine perfections,
Cor Mariae, abyssus gratiae,	Heart of Mary, unfathomable depth of grace,
Cor Mariae, thronus gloriae,	Heart of Mary, throne of glory,
Cor Mariae, abyssus mysteriorum,	Heart of Mary, unfathomable depth of mysteries,
Cor Mariae, soli Deo cognitum,	Heart of Mary, known to God alone,
Cor Mariae, origo totius sanctimoniae sacratissimae Virginis,	Heart of Mary, source of all the Most Sacred Virgin's sanctity,
Cor Mariae, hortus florum caelestium,	Heart of Mary, garden of heavenly flowers,
Cor Mariae super angelicum,	Heart of Mary surpassing the angelic,
Cor Mariae innocentissimum,	Heart of Mary most innocent,
Cor Mariae mitissimum,	Heart of Mary most meek,
Cor Mariae humillimum,	Heart of Mary most humble,
Cor Mariae purissimum,	Heart of Mary most pure,
Cor Mariae obedientissimum,	Heart of Mary most obedient,

Cor Mariae, paradisus evangelicarum Beatitudinum,	Heart of Mary, paradise of the evangelical Beatitudes,
Cor Mariae, gazophylacium Ecclesiae,	Heart of Mary, treasury of the Church's riches,
Cor Mariae, fons lucis et gratiae,	Heart of Mary, fountain of light and grace,
Cor Mariae, sedes misericordiae,	Heart of Mary, seat of mercy,
Cor Mariae, regula cordium fidelium,	Heart of Mary, rule of faithful hearts,
Cor Matris Jesu dignissimum,	Most worthy Heart of the Mother of Jesus,
Cor Matris nostrae studiosissimum,	Most devoted Heart of our Mother,
Propitius esto, *parce nobis, Jesu.*	Be merciful, *spare us, O Jesus.*
Propitius esto, *exaudi nos, Jesu.*	Be merciful, *graciously hear us, O Jesus.*
Per Cor amantissimum Beatissimae Matris tuae, *exaudi nos, Jesu.*	Through the most loving Heart of Thy Most Blessed Mother, *graciously hear us, O Jesus.*
Per summum ejus in Patrem tuum amorem, *exaudi nos, Jesu.*	Through her Heart's supreme love for Thy Father, *graciously hear us, O Jesus.*
Per ardentissimam ejus in te dilectionem, *etc.*	Through her Heart's most ardent love for Thee, *etc.*
Per excellentissimam ejus cum Corde tuo unionem,	Through her Heart's most sublime union with Thine own,

Per specialem ejus erga sibi devotos charitatem,	Through her Heart's special love for those devoted to It,
Per piissima illius desideria,	Through her Heart's most pious desires,
Per omnes purissimos illius affectus,	Through all her Heart's most pure affections,
Per omnes sanctissimos illius motus,	Through all her Heart's most holy movements,
Per acerbissimos dolores ipsius,	Through her Heart's most bitter sorrows,
Per temporalia et aeterna ejus gaudia,	Through her Heart's joys in time and in eternity,
O pretiosissimum Cor Jesu et Mariae, thesaurus cordis nostri, *posside cor nostrum in aeternum.*	O most precious Hearts of Jesus and Mary, treasure of our hearts, *possess our hearts forever.*
O amantissimum Cor Jesu et Mariae, vita cordis nostri, *vive in corde nostro in aeternum.*	O most loving Hearts of Jesus and Mary, life of our hearts, *live in our hearts forever.*
O dilectissimum Cor Jesu et Mariae, Rex cordis nostri, *regna super cor nostrum in aeternum.*	O most beloved Hearts of Jesus and Mary, Sovereigns of our hearts, *reign over our hearts forever.*
Jesu, Cor Mariae, *audi nos.*	Jesus, Heart of Mary, *hear us.*
Jesu, Cor Mariae, *exaudi nos.*	Jesus, Heart of Mary, *graciously hear us.*
Amen.	Amen.

ACT OF REPARATION TO THE SACRED HEART OF JESUS
in the Most Blessed Sacrament

My Savior Jesus Christ, my Master and my God, I adore Thy Sacred Heart behind the veil of the Blessed Sacrament.

I adore this Heart on my own behalf, on behalf of all angels and men, on behalf of all creatures, and especially on behalf and in the place of those who refuse to adore it: demons, blasphemers, the impious, heretics, the indifferent, and all sinners. I adore it as the Heart of my God, as the Heart of the one true living God.

On my own behalf and on behalf of all Thy creatures, I love with all the strength of my heart this most divine, most good, and most adorable Heart, as the living hearth of eternal love, and as the divine and inexhaustible fount of God's mercy, tenderness, and goodness. I love this Heart in the name of all those who have the misfortune to not love it.

O Sacred Heart of Jesus Christ, present and living behind the Eucharistic veils, on my own behalf and on behalf of all creatures, I humbly ask pardon for the countless acts of ingratitude with which the world does not cease to repay Thy prodigious love.

I particularly ask Thy pardon for all sacrileges, all poorly celebrated Masses, all unworthy, bad, or tepid communions, all blasphemies, all mockery and irreverence, and all neglect and lukewarmness to which Thine adorable Sacrament and Thy Divine Heart have been subject since the crime of Judas until today; and in advance, I make reparation for all the outrages of the same kind that will grieve Thy love until the Antichrist and the end of time.

Deign to be merciful to us, O most meek and most clement Heart. I ask Thee in the name of the most holy and immaculate Heart of Thy Blessed Mother, whom Thy filial love has never refused anything. Amen.

CONSECRATION TO THE SACRED HEART OF JESUS

Most adorable, most merciful, and most sacred Heart of my God, I dare to offer Thee and consecrate to Thee my heart. It is, I know, infinitely unworthy of Thee, since Thou art the Heart of the Holy of Holies and it is, alas, but misery, weakness, and sin. However, I trust that Thy mercy will deign to accept the gift of my heart, to be able more effectively to purify, reform, and sanctify it.

I therefore consecrate to Thy Heart, O my beloved Master, all that I am and all that I have, my life and my death, my mind, my judgment, my conscience, my imagination, my will, and my heart with all its affections and sentiments. To Thy Heart I consecrate my body and all my senses, all my words, actions, works, joys, and sufferings; in short, I consecrate and dedicate myself entirely and forever to Thy Sacred Heart.

I happily pledge to honor and adore it all the days of my life, and to make it known, honored, and loved.

Thy Divine Heart, really present with Thy holy humanity in the Eucharist, shall be more than ever my refuge, my repose, my consolation, my hope, and my love. Let it be, O my dear Savior, the supplement to my adoration, thanksgiving, prayers, and penances! Let it be everything to me: light, food, support, abode, grace, and life.

Immaculate Virgin, my sweet and excellent Mother, it is in thy blessed hands that I place this consecration, and it is thee whom I dare charge to keep me, until my last breath, faithful to thy Son, my Divine Master, to Whom be glory and love forever and ever! Amen.

www.ingramcontent.com/pod-product-compliance
Lightning Source LLC
Chambersburg PA
CBHW072200070526
44585CB00015B/1225